Tight Lines

Tales of a flyfishing life

Bill Curry

The Professional Outdoor Media Association of Canada
has awarded *Tight Lines*
FIRST PRIZE
in the Book Category
of its National Communications Awards for 2024

PROFESSIONAL
OUTDOOR MEDIA
ASSOCIATION OF CANADA

Tight Lines: tales of a flyfishing life

Cover image and all interior images, except as noted, by the author
Cover design: Rebekah Wetmore
Author photo: Norma Curry

Editor: Andrew Wetmore

ISBN: 978-1-990187-80-3
First edition May 2023

2475 Perotte Road
Annapolis County, NS
B0S 1A0

moosehousepress.com
info@moosehousepress.com

We live and work in Mi'kma'ki, the ancestral and unceded territory of the Mi'kmaw people. This territory is covered by the "Treaties of Peace and Friendship" which Mi'kmaw and Wolastoqiyik (Maliseet) people first signed with the British Crown in 1725. The treaties did not deal with surrender of lands and resources but in fact recognized Mi'kmaq and Wolastoqiyik (Maliseet) title and established the rules for what was to be an ongoing relationship between nations. We are all Treaty people.

Introduction

Figure 1: Native Nova Scotian brook trout

Last summer, I caught a brook trout in Middle River. For almost fifty years now, this is something I've done most summers.

As I waded the crystal-clear waters of Cape Breton, at the northern end of Nova Scotia, the sound of the river burbling over the stony shingle, mixed with the cries of wheeling eagles overhead and always a distant cowbell clanging on the neck of a steer in the meadow downstream, are magnets that pull me back there.

The brook trout, though, are the main attraction.

As I gazed at the eighteen-inch fish in my hand and gently removed the hook from its mouth, I thought about how this simple act of catching and releasing a large trout was becoming a thing of the past. The blue, black, and red spots on the fish's silver sides—it was a sea-run brook trout, heavy, almost three pounds and full of spunk—shone brightly in the sun. I lowered the trout back into the water, I resolved again to do what I could to make sure my grandson Theo would have this same opportunity.

With the increasing population of the invasive chain pickerel and smallmouth bass in Nova Scotia's waters, the population of native species like the brook trout and the Atlantic salmon has become fewer. Acid rain and the warming global climate have also changed the province's watersheds in ways that the trout and salmon don't like. In fact, the shift is so dramatic that many people believe there is no good brook trout fishing left in Nova Scotia.

They are mistaken, but we need to act now to ensure that is not the case in the future.

~

I was born in New England to a mother whose father believed that, when she married my father from Nova Scotia and eventually moved the family back here, she had been carried off to live in an igloo. To him, Canada was the Far North.

Until we moved permanently to Nova Scotia when I was fifteen, the family summer routine was that we went to stay with my mother's father and her step-mother in Nonquitt, a small, southeastern coastal Massachusetts village almost bordering on Rhode Island. For two or three weeks, we would frolic on the beach and amuse ourselves with camping, swimming, golf, tennis, sailing, and, of course, fishing. A week or so after the Fourth of July weekend, it would be time for the family to travel north to Braebirch, a cottage in Deerfield, Nova Scotia, a small village about a twenty-minute drive from Yarmouth, where the ferry from Bar Harbor, Maine would land us.

Life at the cottage was much less structured than at Nonquitt and focused almost exclusively on Hooper Lake, which the cottage overlooked. We would make the occasional trips to Port Maitland, where we'd visit various members of Dad's family and play on the wonderfully expansive, mile-long sand beach; or to the French Shore beaches at Bartletts or Mavillette.

Most of our time at Braebirch, though, centred on fishing. Fishing has always been a part of my life, something passed on to me by my grandfather, who adored trout fishing, and by my father, a flyfishing enthusiast who also spent most of his time looking for brook trout.

In my family, fishing is something of a lifestyle, not just an activity. Great-uncles who were keen salmon fishermen, uncles who were trout lovers, and other family members, including the women who were married to these fishermen, were all, it seems, nature lovers. My dad, a biologist, passed on this love of the outdoors to me and to my brother, who followed my father's footsteps and became a biology professor. My sister enjoys the outdoors just as much, particularly horseback riding, the love of which she inherited from our mother. And all of our in-laws are "outdoorsy" people, although to a person I suspect we dislike that term. We simply enjoy being in nature, which happens to be outside.

These stories of flyfishing in my family are set mainly in Nova Scotia. They are in a modified chronological order as I remember events, from the mid-1950s through to the present. The stories feature not just the individuals but also the spirit of the people in my life, and always their love for nature, particularly for brook trout. The individual stories recount adventures in my life as a fly fisherman, while the larger narrative emerges of the development of a conservationist.

I am now, in retirement, a professional conservation photographer who records things others may not notice; I make images that reveal things most might not see. I love it when people learn something from my images and when they come to appreciate nature more—also the reason for this book. The stories I grew up with and that I took part in help to show how a child growing up in rural Nova Scotia becomes a naturalist through a love of fishing, particularly flyfishing. The stories in this book are real—but they are fish stories. All anglers will know what that means.

Life has a way of coming full circle. My wife and I now live twenty minutes away from the family property at Deerfield. Our newly-built home overlooks Port Maitland Beach, but on property that has been in the family, off and on, since English settlers from Cape Cod appeared in this part of Nova Scotia in the mid-1700s. The land grant given for our property, which was mapped out in the 1760s, was signed to a relative in 1785. The cemetery next door, which was started when the church group purchased a piece of the property from a relative, has on the deed my great-great-grandfather's signature. They were all, among other things, fisher folk.

So you see, the tradition goes back a long, long time, and follows through to today—I am just steps from a very good flyfishing spot. And that's where the story begins.

Bill Curry

For Theo—the torch is passed

This is a memoir, combined with advice based on decades of study and practical experience. It is accurate to the best of the author's recollections.

Tight Lines

Images

1: A fisherman is born

Figure 2: Tusket River

Baptism was not a concept my family was familiar with, having been raised in the traditions of Unitarian Universalists and Quakers. I was four years old when I became immersed, at the hand of my grandfather and father, in the fine art of fishing.

It may have been that my mother, more cautious when it came to what to allow her children to do, had simply said, "He's not ready yet!" In any case, my father and grandfather took me down to the brook above our lake so that we could fish what our family called the Steer Hole.

As it turned out, my mother's hesitation was immediately validated, and my baptism into the world of fishing was of the full-immersion kind, as I rather incautiously stepped off the small, steep bank, a night crawler in one hand and a small spinning rod in the other. Without a free hand to catch myself on the bank, I demonstrated that Steer Hole was just slightly deeper than the height of a four-year-old child.

Since it was the second week of July, the adult men didn't think such an event warranted the end of our fishing, so they hoisted me out of the stream and placed me on the grassy bank. In later years, I would come to realize that falling in—even by complete immersion standards—was something Curry men and our kin did with a fair degree of regularity. Fortunately, Nova Scotia's generally flat surface means that most rivers are short and relatively shallow, and so a dunking is rarely something to worry about, particularly in the warmth of July and August.

My father, a flyfishing purist, separated himself a bit from my grandfather and me, wandering slightly upstream from us—probably wise, given a four-year-old's sense of distance from a backcast. He left my supervision more to my grandfather, who, as an occasional fly fisherman, would use whatever tactics he felt would work best. In July that meant night crawlers.

I should mention that we had gone out the night before to perform the ritual of collecting night crawlers off the front lawn of our cottage. One could purchase the worms for ten cents a dozen in those days, but then one isn't an "independent fisherman", they told me.

So we waited until dark—which in July is long after when a four-year-old should be in bed—and then out onto the lawn we went. Dad and Grampy were armed with large flashlights, and my job was to hold the bait can, an old soup tin, as they scurried about. Grampy would spotlight a worm, and Dad would drop quickly and try to grab it.

Of course, I tipped the can a few times and they had to remind me to hold it upright, lest I should encourage escapees. In the end, we had about twenty big, juicy worms that trout find irresistible.

There were nice things about fishing a still water like the Steer

Hole: it was narrow, so a young boy didn't have to cast too far, and there was also little current. so the bobber tended to stay put. With Grampy's help, I would eventually get the night-crawler-baited hook out with about a foot and a half of line below the bobber, and then we would wait.

My little spinning rod combo was of the closed-face variety. This was good in that it didn't allow a curious kid to play like a kitten and unwind the entire spool of monofilament, but bad in that any snarls, which inevitably happened, tended to occur inside the covered spool. (My grandfather, a very patient man, as most ministers tend to be, spent much of his time in subsequent fishing outings with me attending to my snarls and helping me "cast" out into the brook.)

The Steer Hole is about a mile above where the Annis River flows out into Hooper Lake in Yarmouth County, Nova Scotia. Our family cottage, built in the late 1800s, had served as a guide's camp, a more remote cabin of the Braemar Lodge outfit—one of the older guest lodges that catered to Americans and other tourists. Our camp, and my uncle's across the brook where the Annis exited Hooper Lake, were used by Babe Ruth and other famous sports figures who frequently fished and hunted the area in the early- to mid-1900s.

You could reach the Steer Hole by a long paddle from the cottage across the lake and up the Annis River, but my dad wisely sensed that such a circuitous route would probably mean a bored little boy by the time we would arrive at our destination. Not that I didn't enjoy a good canoe ride, but a young boy's attention span is such that dragging one's hand in the water and being generally fidgety become more entertaining than sitting still in a canoe, watching the scenery.

This morning, then, we had simply driven the couple of miles around the lake and up the road to where the brook from Lily Pond Brook goes under the road and then meanders out across a pasture before merging with the Annis River proper, forming the Steer Hole, given its name because, well, there were cattle in the pasture. And cattle in Nova Scotia in the late 1950s and early 1960s meant some would surely be steer.

We parked the Jeep Cherokee wagon on the small dirt road that led to Lily Pond and walked carefully along the brook to the Steer Hole. I say *carefully* because my grandfather had a healthy respect for cattle—especially steer. I would later learn that my grandfather's approach to a cow-filled space often included mental calculations as to the proximity of the cattle versus the speed one could make and the direction one might go. The result of these silent observations would dictate whether or not he would attempt a crossing of a bovine-infested area.

One particular steer, owned by a neighbour, was pastured immediately downstream from our property. Unfortunately for my grandfather, this meant the cattle were immediately adjacent to one of the best spots along "our part" of the river.

Once, while fishing this area below our cottage, Grampy crossed the neighbour's pasture to fish a much deeper hole, what the family referred to as Richardson's Pool, so named for the neighbour. Grampy did the required herd/footspeed/distance calculations but missed the mark on the apparent speed of an especially feisty steer. As things happened, he found himself chased out into the water, without his waders on!

I remember to this day the look on my grandfather's face when, much later that same year, our neighbour, Charlie Richardson, came up the road with a package for Grampy. Charlie said, "This is for you, Emerson."

Grampy opened the bundle covered in plain brown paper and saw inside a package of beef in steaks, hamburger, and stew meat, along with a few other choice morsels. "Reverend Chaser" had been processed and packaged, and would become several suppers.

At each of these meals, my grandfather related the tale of being chased into the water!

On the day of my fishing baptism, there were no such encounters with livestock. We settled in worry-free, once Grampy had extracted me from the brook. He propped me up, told me to be more careful, and helped me impale a night crawler, a task that I think hastened my love of flyfishing.

On this first day, though, as on many to come in subsequent years, we baited the worm onto the hook in what we hoped was an attractive manner for the fish, and placed a bobber—a small, round, red-and-white painted plastic one with a little clip pin underneath and a spring-loaded button on top—about two feet up the line.

With my grandfather's aid, I tossed the worm and bobber toward the stream, only to have it snap back and hit me in the chest. I had, and not for the last time, just chucked the bobber and bait toward the water, but was not paying attention to the reel. You see, if you don't hold the button down on a bait casting reel, the line doesn't move!

"Try it again," Grampy said. "Only this time, don't let go of the button on the reel, and let the bobber reach the water."

Doing as I was told on my second attempt, I held down the button on the reel as I cast, let go of the button as the rod came forward, and this time the bait and bobber combination sailed out nicely—landing in the shrubs and weeds about five feet up the bank on the far side of the stream. Retrieving the bobber from the vegetation and then reeling it in across the small stream meant there was no worm left on the hook by the time I was ready to cast again. We would have to sacrifice another night crawler.

As I readied my newly-processed attraction for the trout, I heard from just behind me the voice of my saintly patient ancestor. "Try again. Only this time not so hard!"

The third time was indeed the charm. I managed to lob the bobber and bait instead of whipping the outfit, and the possibly-enticing combination of hook, worm, and bobber landed in the middle of the Steer Hole. With the commotion of the previous cast and retrieve attempts settling down, the two of us watched the small, painted ball bob on the surface of the dark water, and waited.

The Steer Hole proved a good choice for a first fishing experience for a four-year-old as, rather quickly, the bobber began to twitch, then bob up and down, making small concentric circles, which spread out across the stream's mirrored surface.

"Wait until the bobber goes under," Grampy advised, "then pull your rod tip up to hook the fish."

Following his advice as best I could, I waited until the bobber was almost completely submerged and was in fact moving sideways downstream. Then I raised my rod tip. Apparently I did this a bit too forcefully, as not only did I fail to hook the fish, but the worm and bobber ended up clearing my grandfather, who was standing behind me, and sailing into the pasture behind us.

"Good try," Grampy said. "Only you tried to hook him a little too hard."

I reeled in the bobber to half a foot from the rod tip, to find that, of course, there was again no worm on the hook. Grampy, having anticipated as much, was handing me the third unfortunate worm, which I quickly stuck through with the hook.

"Easy does it," Grampy said, a phrase I heard him say often, and not just in fishing circumstances. The advice proved timely, as I probably would have thrown the bait clear to the highway in my frustration if he hadn't warned me. Paying attention to the reel and the trigger button, I managed to ease the float and worm into the middle of the stream with a short but effective cast.

We had to wait longer, probably because the fish were still wondering what had happened with all the previous fuss. After several minutes, which to me felt like an eternity, Grampy said, "Reel in, but only two turns, just enough to move the worm slightly."

I did as instructed and the bobber twitched a little.

"Stop," Grampy said.

The bobber ceased movement, but then twitched, this time not by my doing. The plastic ball was doing a little dance, sending out small waves, but not really going under. Gently this time, I raised my rod tip.

"Good," my grandfather said, "but be patient. Remember, we don't raise the tip until the bobber goes under."

In later years, I would come to realize that flyfishing has another advantage over bait casting: one is constantly casting and retrieving the fly, actually doing something, whereas bait fishing is mostly a waiting game.

As we waited a bit longer, the bobber stopped dancing. Grampy said I should reel in and check to see if I still had a worm.

I did not.

Worm number four was soon in the Steer Hole, suspended beneath the brightly coloured plastic sphere.

Then, it finally happened.

This time, the bobber went down like a periscope on a submarine and was now moving rapidly upstream.

"Raise your tip," I heard from behind me.

I aimed the rod tip skyward, and this time the tip didn't follow immediately; the rod, in fact, began to create an arc.

"You're into one!" Grampy exclaimed, "Now reel in carefully."

The little spinning rod bent almost double—it was a rather cheap rod and reel outfit my dad had bought for me in one of the Yarmouth hardware stores. The fish was now moving back downstream, toward my grandfather and me, and I reeled furiously.

"Easy does it," I heard again.

As the fish swam past us, its back fin broke the plane of the water's surface. We could see the fish was a brook trout, as its spots shone brightly in the dappled sunlight.

"It's a good one," Grampy said.

Somehow, I managed to reel in enough to actually turn the fish back toward us in what was, I am certain now, sheer beginner's luck.

As if out of nowhere, Grampy produced his trout net and had the bamboo handle shoved out toward the brook as he submerged the mesh just behind the trout. With one deft manoeuvre, Grampy swept under the fish and came forward, then up, with the long handle.

My first brook trout was nestled in the woven net. Grampy quickly brought it ashore.

He yelled over to my dad, "Bill got his first fish!"

Dad was already most of the way to us, as the commotion had given away what was occurring, and he wanted to be in on the event.

Grampy placed the trout carefully on the grass. The trout had deeply swallowed the worm. He said, "Guess we'll keep this one."

I was thrilled, as I knew that first fish often went back in the river as a sort of homage to nature, but that an injured fish, like this one, would be kept.

"Yes," my dad said. "It looks to be about nine inches—that will make a nice breakfast trout!"

My grandfather gave a small, pained look, as he didn't actually care for the taste of trout, although my grandmother did. Dad, Mom, my brother, and I loved to eat trout, so I had a broad grin on my face as Dad made this announcement.

"Bill, watch me, and I'll show you how to take care of a trout you're going to keep," he said.

I'd seen Dad fish before, and had watched as he released fish, which is what he preferred to do, keeping only a few each season for an occasional feed of trout, but it hadn't occurred to me that something different would happen when one wished to keep a trout. With a quick but sure hand, Dad placed his thumb under the trout's jaw, and his index and middle fingers slightly into the fish's gills below its head, and then he pulled upward and back. The trout ceased movement as its neck was instantly broken.

"It's not fair to let them suffer if you're going to keep them," Dad said, "so I always kill them quickly. Get some moss from the edge of the brook and we'll put this one in the creel."

I quickly gathered two handfuls of moss from the stream's edge. Dad was dipping the trout in the water to wash it off.

"Look at the gorgeous colours," he said as he handed me the fish, "the beautiful reds and blues."

I was transported from the slight sense of loss I had felt when Dad killed the trout to a feeling of awe as I examined the beautiful brook trout that was my first "caught on my own" prize. I placed the moss in the creel, a handmade wicker basket that Grampy had bought from a local Mi'kmaq fellow who lived in a tepee near the Raynardton Road, and then gently put the trout in on top.

"That will help keep it fresh until we get home," Dad said.

I don't remember catching any more fish myself that day, although as a group we must have, because later, Dad showed me how to clean a trout, cutting off the head and then taking out the stomach and entrails, and how to get one ready to cook.

The next morning, Mom cooked some bacon in one of the several Lodge cast iron frying pans we owned, while Dad showed me how to roll the trout in cornmeal. When the bacon was done and removed from the pan, we placed the trout into the leftover bacon fat and cooked it for about seven minutes a side.

The smell of the bacon and the browning fish was heavenly, and to know I had actually caught one—Dad had kept track of which one—was thrilling.

When the trout were done, we each got one. I had "my" fish.

We each put a fork under the backbone, but over the flesh, near the front end of our trout and pulled up the bone, which left the flesh from the other side of the trout on the plate. Flipping the fish over in our hands, we did the same thing and thus removed the entire backbone in a two-step process. A little salt and pepper were on hand, but not really necessary, and I had my first taste of my own hand-caught brook trout.

The trout were not the only things hooked from that experience.

2: BFF: before flyfishing

Figure 3: Salmon River

My brother Bob, two years younger than me, has been a constant in my fishing adventures. His development as a fly fisherman, not surprisingly, parallels mine in many respects. So Bob's first trout was an experience similar to mine, without the drama of baptism by immersion, which shows that Dad and Grampy were nothing if not consistent—one might say even traditional.

On a warm day in late July, Dad took us over to one of the family's favourite fishing holes, the spot we call The Culvert. The Culvert is, quite simply, a spot on the Tusket River where a side brook flows rather unceremoniously—almost inconspicuously to non-fishing types—under a two-lane dirt road and into what is now known as Lake Vaughn.

Lake Vaughn is a man-made water feature, the result of Nova Scotia Power damming the Tusket River about two miles up from its estuary to create a power project, which began in 1929 after a smaller project, started in 1908, burned down in 1921. Although the power dam had a fish ladder, which was designed to allow Atlantic salmon, sea trout, and other anadromous fish passage through the power system, old-timers say the dam was one factor in the demise of the Atlantic salmon, which have been all but extirpated from most of southwest Nova Scotia. My father, normally a non-violent person, often said that, given two sticks of dynamite and the chance to use them anywhere he'd like, he would put both under that dam!

In the days before the dam, my great-uncle Roy, who was married to my grandfather's half-sister Alice, used to guide close friends and family to the best salmon and trout fishing on the Tusket, and often it was within sight of his small cabin in Raynardton. Today, Lake Vaughn not only rarely has any Atlantic salmon, but it is also rare to catch a trout in the lake proper. Trout can still be found in the small tributaries—trout that have escaped are the reason for the limited populations of cold-water fish in the lake. You see, Lake Vaughn is now crammed full of smallmouth bass and chain pickerel.

In 1962, Lake Vaughn held large numbers of perch, both white and yellow, shiners, eels, and some very nice brook trout. This day in the middle of the summer and at two in the afternoon, we had complete cloud cover, with a faint south wind—perfect conditions for two young boys and their dad to enjoy some fun fishing. A south wind was perfect, as my grandfather always proclaimed, "Wind from the east, fish bite least."

Much later, my daughter, as an eight-year-old, would add, "Wind from the west, fish bite best, wind from the south, catch them in the mouth." But that intelligence was not something my brother and I had discerned at the time. Besides, it seemed the chant, recited each time we went fishing, didn't really matter much. It wasn't as if Dad and Grampy weren't going to go fishing if the wind was east, just that they'd have the excuse ready for a poor catch!

The water was slick, with only a slight breeze, as The Culvert is protected from south winds, making the spot all the more attractive for teaching youngsters to fish. The water was also quite low, so that meant Bob and I would have to fish on the lake side while sitting on top of the large boulders that formed the shoulder of the highway and protected the dirt road from falling into the lake and the middle of The Culvert from washing away in a freshet.

Dad set up both of us with night crawlers, and I, being the experienced seven-year-old that I was, helped Bob cast his outfit. Dad, seeing the rare co-operative spirit, took advantage of the occasion to flick a Mickey Finn streamer into the flow as it went into the lake, but he didn't raise anything.

Bob and I were intrigued by a shiner I caught, and I caught a couple of yellow perch as well. Perch have a sort of sinister look, with sharp, pointy fins, and so aren't really pleasant to touch. They're not as bad as slimy eels but something to handle with respect, while the shiner was smooth and pretty, and fun to touch.

Just as the wind began to pick up and shift slightly west, our grandfather pulled up in his jet-black Chevy sedan. Grampy got out and immediately threw his own Mickey Finn into the current as it ran under the road. Great excitement ensued as he quickly rose a nice trout, but missed it in the end.

Seeing that Bob and I already had worms set to go, my "whatever works" Grampy asked Bob if he'd like some help. Bob's hook was promptly baited with a fresh, large night crawler and cast out just past where Grampy had risen the fish.

Almost immediately the bobber "popped" and went underwater, the fish nailing the worm on the first pass. When Bob raised the tip, his small rod arced beautifully as the fish ran out into the lake.

Dad came over and encouraged Bob in the playing of the fish, and Grampy, net ever-ready, swooped the trout in one try as it ran toward The Culvert, and was heading upstream.

That was Bob's first "on his own" brook trout. It yielded a nine-and-a-half-inch gorgeous fish, once again a trout that had inhaled the worm deeply enough that it was quickly declared "a breakfast fish."

Over the next six years, that scenario was pretty typical of our trout-fishing trips with Dad and Grampy Curry. Dad would take the two of us out to a spot, like the meadow and bridge near our cottage, and we'd all fish together, with us boys getting better and better at making a good-looking worm setup and better and better at casting with the bait rods.

Dad would get us settled in a place where he knew there were fish; if the situation was right, he might take a few casts with his own fly rod nearby.

One evening, he set up the two of us just above a small bridge, then moseyed upriver about twenty-five yards. I missed a small trout, and all three of us then moved upstream with little else showing.

Dad rose a small trout on a Silver Doctor before Bob and I were even with him in the next pool, but as I arrived right after Dad and witnessed the rise, I was then ready. Ready to poach a nice little seven-and-a-half inch fish right out from under Dad's nose.

Graciously, he allowed that we could keep that one, as it had been a slow day. So we dispatched the fish and placed it with care in the creel. I kept opening the basket to check on my prize, but Bob fished a bit more intently.

When Dad declared we would have to head home, Bob said he'd prefer to stay and keep trying for a trout as he didn't want eggs for breakfast.

The next morning at breakfast, I shared my trout so that everyone, including my two-year-old sister, got a bite. The good feeling of having provided fish for the crowd was not lost on me.

Over the next couple of years, my brother and I would fish almost daily while we were at the cottage in Deerfield. Hooper Lake at that time was similar to Lake Vaughn, having been dammed until the late 1950s by a small wood mill just below the lake outlet, across the river from our cottage property. The mill had stopped operating and was in slow decay throughout the 1960s and 1970s, a place young kids were forbidden to enter. Since the gate had been long ago dismantled, the dam really had little impact on the water level in the lake.

At that time, the lake held prized fish; brook trout, and a small number of brown trout that had been introduced in the 1940s. There were Atlantic salmon that would run up the Annis River, which was not completely dammed like the Tusket, but, being a much smaller watershed, it didn't have nearly the capacity of the larger river. In the spring, the gaspereaux (or *kiacks* as they were called locally; alewives in scientific terms) would ascend the river, as did eels. The lake had horned pout, a small version of what a Southerner might more properly call a brown catfish, and there were perch in abundance, both the white and the yellow species.

Our fishing for these first few years was the "off the dock" variety. Mom and Dad kept watch while we scrambled around the small stone pier that jutted out into the lake in front of the cottage. Our fishing improved immeasurably in those days when our cousins would come to visit because, while Jim, who was older than Bob and me, didn't care for fishing, his brother Don, who was just a couple of years older than me, loved to fish and enjoyed Deerfield's piscatorial offerings as much as we did. Don's dad, our uncle Don, who was married to Dad's sister Phyllis, was as keen a fly fisherman as my dad, and would become a huge influence in my destiny as a fly fisherman and much later in my professional career. So, while the girls—my sister, Lisa, and cousins Linda and Susan—stood at the shore, throwing rocks and undertaking other amusements, we "men" fished.

When I was about nine years old and Bob was seven, we were given our own little plastic boats. For a few years, these vessels would be the height of entertainment and increased dramatically our fishing experiences and education about fishing.

The boats require some explanation, as I've never seen any since, most likely because, like other 1960s fads such as lawn darts, a manufacturer nowadays would shy away from the liabilities related to them!

Bob and I had gone to camp each summer during the time we visited Grampy Carl and Aboo (my mom's father and his wife) on the Massachusetts coast just south of Cape Cod. Camp Nonquitt included a vast array of water-based activities, but in order to access them on your own, you had to pass the "water test." The test, essentially, was to swim the length of the large swimming pier at the beach, and then tread water for three to five minutes.

The swim part, maybe fifty to seventy-five yards, was easy. Treading water, enough so that one could also be heard singing, "Mary Had a Little Lamb" repeatedly, was tough. We eventually both passed the test so we could go sailing and use the paddle boats—small wooden punts propelled by straight-shafted kayak-type paddles.

The camp experience proved to Mom and Dad that we could be trusted in small craft, and the plastic boats were the smallest of small craft.

The boats—our parents bought a pair of them, one for each boy (my sister got a pony, but that's a whole other story)—were about four feet long and almost as wide. Made out of fairly hard and stiff blue plastic, they defined personal watercraft in the early 1960s.

They were propelled by hand, as in hand paddling over the side. They could be flipped over, and we could then scare the crap out of our mother, say, as she would see us disappear, but we could come up under the overturned vessel and breathe quite nicely, chuckling to ourselves for the wittiness of the trick.

In those days, PFD meant "parental foresight demanded": the only protection we had were firm rules about where, when, and how far we could take the boats out into the lake.

What is most important to know about these boats is that they made excellent fishing platforms. Armed with a bait can and some worms—night crawlers preferred, but since we needed lots of them for "serious" fishing with the grown-ups, we also used garden worms dug out of Grampy's vegetable garden—and the ubiquitous small rod and reel and bobber, we were really quite ready to fish. And now quite mobile.

The apex of our BFF (before flyfishing) experience would be the end-of-summer tournament played yearly from our blue boats on Hooper Lake. The rules for the tournament were quite simple: each participant got points for fish caught. It was a sliding scale with perch, horned pout, and other small fish like shiners worth one point each, and trout worth five points each.

One year toward the end of the tournament's run, and as we learned more about flyfishing, the rules were changed to allow that brook trout should be worth five points and brown trout worth only three, but that rule was never actually employed.

The contest would take place with both boats launched simul-taneously and parental rules still strictly enforced. The contest would end when one of us caught an eel.

This last rule was the result of two factors. First, we both were wary of eels and normally eels would take the bait so deeply that, in order to get one off the hook, we'd have to break the line and simply cut the eel loose. The second factor was that neither of us wanted an eel in the small boat with us!

The whole eel aversion was a bit of an education anyway. One day in a pre-tournament practice, Bob caught a large eel. We dragged it ashore and found that indeed it had swallowed the worm way down its gut, much too far to get hold of with our little pliers.

The solution, of course, was that we would have to clean out the eel by killing it and then retrieving the hook. We decided the best thing to do was take it to the woodshed and use Dad's axe to cut its head off and get the hook out. Such is the logic of a pair of pre-teen nimrods.

I've referred to the conservation ethic that my entire family ob-serves, and our choice of location and method of execution of the poor eel led to a family lesson. Unbeknownst to us, our grandpar-ents had arrived and were conversing with Mom in the kitchen while Dad was mowing the lawn and absent-mindedly watching us.

My maternal grandmother, an English war bride who came to Canada with Grandfather after World War One, spotted Bob and me as we were tussling with the eel, the chopping block, and the axe. She summoned Dad quickly and said "George, have those two got an eel? How lovely!"

Grammy Curry had Dad relieve us of the eel, and then she proceeded to show us how to clean it (she did give us back the hook) and prepare it for the frying pan.

How frying two species of fish can be so different, I still don't fully understand: while frying trout look and smell wonderful, the sight of that eel still squirming as if alive in the hot pan, and the smell...well, let's just say neither procurer of the eel was thrilled to be subjected to tasting the resulting dish.

As an adult, I quite like smoked eel, but I suppose that is because they are never wriggling dead in a pan and there's no wood smoke.

In any case, Grammy declared the eel quite tasty. I believe she was alone in that opinion!

~

The years went by, and Bob and I fished a lot and learned still more about nature and the flora and fauna of Nova Scotia. Dad was as patient a teacher as Grampy, and Dad enjoyed talking to us about the plants and animals that shared our habitat. He was also careful to never take us out so long that we were bored.

If the fishing was slow, he'd often go into teaching mode and show us things like pitcher plants and how they trapped water and food in their cup-shaped blooms, or show us beaver workings and comment on the need for beaver to always be chewing.

The four to six weeks we spent every summer in Nova Scotia was a time of play and wonder. We had a large group of local kids who would come swim in the lake with us, who read and exchanged comic books with us, and who camped out with us, and a couple of the boys would go fishing with us from time to time as well. Occasionally, friends of Mom and Dad's would come to Nova Scotia with their children, like our two sets of neighbours in Massachusetts, who also had three kids each, of about the same age.

It was a wonderful time for learning about nature, for communing with the rivers and lakes. The call of the loons still thrills me, as it did then. The other waterfowl that shared the lake and the rivers we fished were always highlights of any trip, as any animals would be, such as the beaver or muskrat that we frequently encountered.

We caught a lot of trout and became keen fishermen. We also became keenly aware of the natural surroundings and the beauty of an unspoiled province. When we got to fish with Dad and Grampy and other adult relatives, we were invited into a club that was special. We were joining those who have a respect and love for the outdoors, where trout once abounded.

3: A flyfishing addiction begins

Figure 4: The author (l) and his brother, Bob. Photo by their dad.

I don't know why Dad waited so long to teach us flyfishing, as he was rather a "purist" about his fishing. He did use a casting rod when he fished for striped bass, using colourful wooden plugs or live bait suspended beneath balloons, which were a gigantic version of the bobbers and worms we used, with mackerel in place of night crawlers.

Aside from his saltwater fishing, Dad really preferred to use a fly. I suppose because bait fishing is so easy and my brother and I obviously enjoyed it so much, Dad simply let good things be good things and didn't want to push his approach on us.

Bob and I had seen Dad flyfishing, of course, both in New England and more particularly on the summer trips to Nova Scotia. When the family went to Vermont to open or close up our ski chalet, Dad often took a fly rod along and would fish the small, shallow, narrow streams near Londonderry and Weston. Because the streams were so small, they were not good for bait-equipped boys so, even when we accompanied Dad on his brief fishing trips there, we would find more entertainment making small boats out of scrap wood, complete with sails made of sticks and leaves or litter, which we would sail gloriously downstream, with Dad flyfishing upstream, of course. Nothing puts fish down quicker and raises a fly fisherman's ire quicker than a miniature version of the schooner *Bluenose* swirling through a pool! (Well, almost nothing —but that is another story.)

It was during our yearly sojourn to the cottage in Nova Scotia where we witnessed Dad in his flyfishing element. He would flyfish daily along the flowing river that bordered our property as it went out of Hooper Lake, past my uncle's cottage across the river, down past the old mill dam, made a sharp U at Richardson's Pool, and then doubled back and flowed toward the next lake downstream, Lake Ellenwood.

~

Dad and his adult group of fishermen enjoyed an annual May trip to Nova Scotia. The routine was that Dad and four or five of his buddies would take off from Massachusetts on the long weekend in May—the US long weekend, Memorial Day, not the Canadian long weekend, Victoria Day—and they'd drive to Bar Harbor, Maine, to catch the Bluenose ferry that ran three times weekly in the off-season from Bar Harbor to Yarmouth, Nova Scotia.

They'd stop at L.L. Bean on the way up, of course—in our family it would be considered very strange indeed not to stop in at Bean's, which was founded by a distant cousin, to check out the latest and greatest in fishing gear and especially to load up on trout flies.

During the six-hour crossing of the Bay of Fundy, the men would chat excitedly about where they'd fish and what spots they thought would be good given the water conditions that year. The group would use our cottage as their fishing base, a purpose for which the cottage was designed and built.

Even in the 1960s, though, the quality of trout fishing in Nova Scotia was beginning to decline. Although the fishing around the cottage was still easy, the fish were smaller and less numerous. Accessible pools were beginning to be "fished out"; some years, Dad's group would really have to work to catch much.

Later, scientists would ascribe much of this change to the beginning impact of acid rain, but to the men in Dad's group it only meant one thing: they'd have to go farther afield.

For years, Dad's group had simply fished the "easy" pools quite near the larger rivers' outflows, pools like the ones my great-uncle Roy had shown them on the lower reaches of the Tusket River, and the pools adjacent to roads leading a bit further into the province's interior, such as Highway 203 that, in those days, went in to the fire tower at Kempt and past that became more an ox path than a road through to the town of Shelburne.

Nova Scotia is known for its "accessible wilderness." The province was settled by sea-fishing folk; lobster, scallops and groundfish comprising important parts of the economy. This meant that while the coast was quite populated for much of its length, the interior of the province remained for the most part unsettled and was true wilderness.

This holds true to this day. There are two wilderness national parks in Nova Scotia—Kejimkujik National Park and the adjacent Tobeatic Wilderness Area—which cover much of the interior in the southwest area of the province (the area touching Digby, Yarmouth, Shelburne, and Queens counties), and Cape Breton Highlands National Park, situated at the northern end of the province.

In Dad's investigations for better fishing spots, he'd heard of some very good trout fishing in Quinan and area. Driving the rough road into the area, Dad and the group were fortunate to meet a man of Acadian descent Pierre Vacon, who went by his anglicized name, Peter.

~

The Quinan area is home to a population of folks of Acadian ancestry. The ancestors of the residents were for the most part the French people who had settled the area originally in the very early 1600s, but who had been deported in the Expulsion of 1755, when the British who governed Nova Scotia at that time decided that all Acadians who refused to take the Oath of Allegiance posed a threat to the Crown and should be removed. Longfellow wrote an epic poem titled "Evangeline" about this event.

Many of the deported Acadians ended up in Louisiana, where they became known as Cajuns, while some eventually made their way back to Nova Scotia. The British, anticipating the return of some Acadians, circulated advertisements in Massachusetts saying that anyone who wished could simply come as settlers and get free land.

In 1761, the towns of Yarmouth and Barrington were born when a large group of settlers from Cape Cod took up the offer. Later, upon finding the best land already cultivated by English settlers, any returning Acadians moved back in as near as they could to their former farms, and for many that meant places like the Pubnicos and Wedgeport, Tusket and Quinan.

Some of the ancestors of residents in the Quinan area, as in other areas nearby, never left; instead, they hid in the woods, some intermarrying with Mi'kmaq inhabitants, and stayed until the British lost interest in uprooting the Acadians.

An interesting side note to this abridged history: the Expulsion and the subsequent settling of the southwest end of the province by folks from Cape Cod explains why Yarmouth and Shelburne Counties of Nova Scotia have some of the highest concentrations of Mayflower descendants outside of New England: the vast majority of those who took the British up on the free land offer were May-flower descendants themselves. With the scarcity of land in the Plymouth area and nearby Sandwich and beyond on Cape Cod, the entrepreneurial spirit of these people perhaps led them to be more willing to risk resettlement.

~

Peter Vacon proved to be a wonderful guide. He had guided Babe Ruth and many other famous sporting figures for both hunting and fishing.

When he met Dad's group for the first time, he quickly accepted the day's wage and took them into an area now known as Cold-stream, about three miles back from Quinan proper. The men had a great day's flyfishing, taking many small trout in the freshet running into the Tusket River from the Coldstream Brook.

The group didn't keep many fish, preferring to catch and release, but the morning on Coldstream and the afternoon's subsequent canoe paddle into a couple of the lakes nearby, paired with the superb flyfishing for larger brook trout, convinced the men that this was the way fishing was supposed to be.

The experience also gave Dad an idea.

~

Christmas the year I was twelve included some packages that weren't much of a surprise to either my brother or me. We each received a gift that was wrapped in a rather, shall we say, casual manner, indicating Dad had done the wrapping. The packages were cylindrical, about four feet long and thin in diameter.

Instantly we knew these would be new fishing rods, but had no idea what kind of life-changing instruments would be inside.

The unwrapped gifts told us that Dad had obviously gone to L. L. Bean and had procured for each of us a brand-new fly rod. Other gifts that morning included fly-reels and flyfishing vests and other assorted paraphernalia one would need to go flyfishing, including, of course, a small selection of trout flies.

The Christmas gifts were part of a rather elaborate setup. Dad would undertake to teach the two of us to cast a fly rod during the spring and summer, and then, in late August, the three of us would have an adventure: we'd go flyfishing with Peter Vacon!

Bob and I were very excited at the idea. It seemed as if we were being invited into the flyfishing faction—a faction we both had observed and had looked forward to joining.

The summer came, and in mid-July we drove to Bar Harbor, Maine to take the ferry. Of course, along the way we stopped at Bean's. Bob and I both bought flies, having anticipated this side trip to Freeport, Maine, where L. L. Bean was the town's biggest employer and tourist draw.

When we arrived at the cottage, Dad began a joyful regimen of teaching us to fly-fish. Our casting lessons were a lot of fun. We practised "on the water," Dad taking us to places like Big Meadow or The Hedge, the main feature of such spots being an open area for both the forward cast and the back cast. The old "Ten o'clock, two o'clock" was drilled into us, with the idea that your back cast had to stop to allow the line to straighten out, and the forward cast similarly had to stop to avoid slapping one's fly too heavily onto the water in front.

I know I didn't catch a thing, but we had great fun nonetheless, and we were constantly thinking ahead to the grand adventure.

Dad taught us how to tie on flies using the clinch knot, and how to tie on a leader using a double surgeon's knot. He did the more precise task of tying the leader to the fly line, but other than that we pretty much learned how to fend for ourselves.

We already knew the names of many of the flies, and we were becoming familiar with a whole new way to fish, a way that depends on getting the fish to hit an artificial fly rather than a live worm.

That summer, I also learned that Steve, one of my friends and a neighbour who lived in the Deerfield area, had a dad, Don, who tied his own flies, and he had taught Steve how to do this. When I went over to Steve's house and explained that Bob and I were going to go flyfishing with our dad, Don got out his fly-tying gear and showed me how to make a black Wooly Bugger with a red tail. He let me keep it as my first hand-tied fly. I was thrilled.

Dad had done some fly-tying, but I think he preferred to purchase the flies as they were not all that expensive. A neighbour in Massachusetts had gone in with Dad to buy a large quantity of flies from a manufacturer.

I loved watching Don tie his flies, as he showed me the various ways to attach feather and material to a hook; I was mesmerized by the whole process. I hadn't even caught a trout on a fly yet, but already I was falling madly in love with the sport just getting ready for it!

When August finally arrived, the fall rains came early; from the middle of the month on, it seemed we got heavy rain frequently. We knew the flyfishing trip was going to require a stretch of good weather, as it would be a long walk to where Peter was going to take us.

We waited with fingers crossed until the appointed day, and the weather gods smiled on us, promising three days of sunshine with some clouds and a west wind! I say "the appointed day" but in reality that would be the day before as we had to prepare our gear, get everything together, including a lunch we'd take with us. Preparations the day before made us all the more anxious for the next morning's departure.

Dad rousted the two of us out of bed at 5 am. We had a quick breakfast of cold cereal, and piled into the old Jeep Wagoneer, which we had loaded the night before with all our equipment.

The drive to Quinan, where we were to meet Peter, was full of excited chatter as we were transported to an experience we had been anticipating for half a year. We all were excited, and Dad I'm sure was hoping that the fishing would be good so the experience would stimulate our interest in flyfishing, and thus in the brook trout and their environs.

The plan was that Peter would drive with us to a place known locally as Meat Rock. The road, in those days, went past Coldstream to Meat Rock and then simply ended and became a walking trail. There were no all-terrain vehicles, or ATVs, in those days, and it's worth noting Bob and I had both done long hikes before with Dad, but this would be a real test.

Peter had a camp on a piece of water that flowed from the very centre of the province to eventually join the Clyde River and enter the Atlantic near Port Clyde in Shelburne County. He used the camp for both hunting and fishing, and its location, on Bloody Creek, was such that it would be an almost five-mile hike each way from Meat Rock. We would stay overnight at the camp, and then trek back out the next day.

At least, that was the plan.

We picked up Peter as scheduled, and found him to be a warm and witty man indeed. We drove to Meat Rock in the Jeep, having it in four-wheel drive mode most of the way once we left the pavement as the back road was wet and slick due to all the rain.

Arriving at Meat Rock, we unloaded the car and Peter hoisted a pack onto his back. He'd brought food for the four of us for that night and the next morning. He had told us that the camp had sleeping accommodations and cooking utensils, so we only needed to carry our fishing gear and a lunch, which, given the age of us younger participants, was probably a good thing.

Thus equipped, we started off into the woods.

Along the way, Peter began to tell some of the most wonderful and complicated stories of the woods that one could imagine. He told a particularly memorable tale of the man who, while moose hunting, grew tired of paddling his canoe, so when the man saw a moose swimming in the lake, he paddled after it. Once he was close enough, the man lassoed the moose about the antlers and, tying the rope to the bow of the canoe, allowed the beast to tow him across the lake, the idea being that when the moose found land on the far side, the man would shoot it and bring it back in the canoe. The plan, according to Peter, went awry when the moose found ground a bit earlier than the hunter anticipated and, as the man stood up to fire, the moose lurched forward, dumping the man out of the canoe. He was left sitting on the mossy bank while he watched the moose run into the woods with the canoe trailing behind, still attached to his antlers. The canoe was destroyed and little pieces could still be found throughout the woods.

With a sense of timing that would do George Carlin proud, we walked by a piece of an old canoe just off the path. "Look, there's some of it now," Peter said.

The moose tale was followed by stories of how the Mi'kmaq residents cooked moose and how they caught them in pits—the former probably true, the latter, well... He told us that, to catch a moose, you put spikes in the bottom of a pit and made a fire among the spikes, and then you'd plant peas around the edge of the ditch. Moose, being fond of vegetables, would come to take the peas, and that's when you'd kick them in the ash-hole! The two of us boys were enraptured!

Story after story made the walk go by quickly. Far-fetched tales of trout tied to logs to attract other trout, or of how to catch a rabbit using pepper, a carrot, and a log (you put pepper on a carrot under a log, the rabbit comes and sniffs and then sneezes, and knocks himself out by the loosened log hitting him on the head) and other tall tales of the woods flowed naturally from the experienced woodsman. He also imparted a lot of accurate woods lore, such as proudly showing us the claw marks that bears had made on rocks when they overturned stones looking for grubs underneath. The positive proof that black bears were in the area would play a key role later that day.

One story I'm certain he didn't plan but that made quite the impact was when Peter spotted a spruce grouse sitting in a branch just above the trail. He said, "Look, they sit so still, they call them Fool Hens because they're so tame."

Bob, presumably thinking this was another tall tale and expecting a stuffed toy, poked at the bird with his fly rod tip. All of us, but most particularly Bob, were astonished when the bird flew off with startlingly loud wingbeats into the thick woods.

We soon arrived at Bloody Creek.

The day was perfect for flyfishing. It was partially overcast, so the sun's brightness was muted most of the time by a light cover of fluffy clouds. There was a gentle west breeze, just enough to slightly ripple the water's surface, which was good because it would help to prevent us fly-fishers from spooking the trout. But the wind was not so much that it would interfere with a novice caster's attempts.

The meandering brook was not very wide, maybe twenty to thirty feet across, so that we wouldn't have to cast far to cover the water. The river's flow was steady enough that it could carry a fly in a downstream direction at a fairly good speed.

The ground near the brook was soggy and mossy, slightly mushy underfoot, but none of us had waders; the intention was to fish off the bank. The meadow the brook cut through was filled with flowers and low growth, and the nearest tree was perhaps fifty yards back, where we'd entered the meadow. The smell of the marshy soil and the scent of the wildflowers and evergreens mixed to create a wonderful aroma, one that is now familiar to me but that was then unknown. It was about ten in the morning, and the dew was still on the plants, which meant that the meadow had a pretty, gleaming quality to it.

As we approached the bank and could see into the brook itself, we caught sight of the dark, sun-dappled, tea-coloured water, and could see the rings made by trout rising to take insects off the film of the water. In short, you could not ask for a more ideal spot to initiate someone into flyfishing.

Dad helped Bob and me set up our gear. He hadn't even pulled out his rod yet, he was so intent on giving us the action. On my first cast, a small trout swished past my fly but didn't hit it.

Dad said, "Retrieve the fly slowly like I showed you, and when you see the rise, raise your rod tip firmly."

I cast again. My little fly, a Parmachene Belle I'd bought from Bean's, landed right where I'd wanted, in the middle of the stream, just beside a rock that was making a little eddy form behind it on my side of the waterway. I retrieved with a small pull on the fly line and immediately a trout whacked at the fly!

I raised my tip, the rod began to arc exquisitely, and I felt the tug as the trout went downstream below the rock. I managed to turn it back upstream by putting some force on the rod.

I heard Dad say, "Easy does it, take your time."

With some effort, I managed to actually get the fly line to the point where I could use my reel—this first flyfishing-hooked trout was a dandy! I reeled a bit and the trout would pull out line, making the reel give a loud phzzzz sound. As I reeled back in, the reel would make a little clicking sound as the spool turned.

The trout and I were engaged like this for a couple of minutes until Peter came alongside me and said, "Would you like me to net it for you?" Not being experienced in having a guide, I was expecting my grandfather's usual "swoop" with a dip net. It hadn't occurred to me that a guide would ask what I might like.

"Yes, please," I said.

Peter immediately reached down with a short-handled trout net which had a large woven black bag made of tightly knotted strings so that the holes in the bag were much smaller than those in the net Grampy had. The trout was swimming back up toward me, partially on its side, tiring, so when Peter got the net to it, he came from behind and under the trout, quickly netting it.

The trout was a beauty.

The glistening water on its sides showed the myriad spots of blue, red, and black. The tail had a white edge, as did all the fins on its stomach. The jaw was slightly hooked. This was a breeding adult male, about sixteen inches long, and was thick so it must have weighed close to two pounds!

I looked at the trout in the net and watched intently as Peter took the hook out of its mouth.

"We'll catch some trout today," he said, "but this is a nice one. Do you want to keep it?"

Worried, I looked at Dad, as I knew he didn't like to keep many uninjured fish.

"That's a nice fish, Bill," Dad said. "Since it's your first on a fly, we'll keep it, and you can show him off to Mom."

I felt a sense of relief. This meant I'd have to quickly kill the fish, which I did, but the beauty of that fish was striking as I rinsed it carefully in a puddle next to the brook and then placed it in the creel with some moss.

Bob had reeled in his fly. He'd only made a cast or two when I hooked my fish. He was standing beside me now. "Nice fish," he said.

"Look, there's a nice rise there," Peter said, pointing at the brook.

Bob hurried over, and Peter showed him where to cast. On the first cast, Bob's fly, a Professor, was smacked so hard the fly went right under the fish that had turned over and actually come down on it! Bob's reel screamed loudly as the line went zipping out; he was into a fish that was practically a twin of mine.

That morning Bob, Dad, and I caught well over fifty fish, and released most, keeping nine. Bob and I each kept four, the two big fish and two others almost identical to the first two, maybe an inch shorter, and then two others each that we had hurt by hooking too deeply. Dad kept one that he had hooked and hurt, as eventually he did some fishing of his own, although not until Bob and I were well up into the dozens of fish caught.

In those days, the limit was fifteen trout each. We could have come out with the three of us hauling forty-five trout. My father's conservation ethic was clearly in evidence here.

And I remember we gladly learned how to release the fish quickly, by holding the hook and not the fish and letting the trout slide back into the water without taking the fish all the way out, so as not to stress it any more than necessary.

The flyfishing kept up at a good pace until, eventually, the trout became less willing and the sun was a bit higher in the sky. It also became less breezy, so the brook was now as smooth as glass. While we could see the rises clearly, the trout became more cautious about our offerings.

It was early afternoon, and Dad suggested we go to the camp to check out the accommodations and to eat lunch. It sounded like a great idea.

Peter's hunting camp was nearby, in a little clearing overlooking the top of the meadow pool we had just been fishing. It was small, maybe sixteen by twenty feet with one small window on the side facing the brook and meadow, and had a large doorway that was open as we approached. The camp had an old picnic table out front that had definitely seen better days and a set of rickety-looking stairs leading up to the door, and the whole building perched on cinder blocks to keep it off the ground. As we came near, a porcupine scuttled off from underneath the back of the building.

Going up the stairway to the camp, we immediately were hit with the smell. Odours of old bacon fat, mould, mouse droppings, and a smell we didn't know but were soon informed was bear fat, all mixed together to form a pungent barrier as we entered.

The interior was just as shocking. There were two single beds low to the floor and a pair of bunk beds against the far wall. The source of the mouldy smell was surely the bedding, which had been nests not only for sports but also for mice and other small mammals. The old mattresses were covered with grey wool blankets, which also had quite the stench—damp wool mixed with lingering smoke and food smells. There was a pillow on each bed, the old striped kind with no niceties such as a pillowcase, and each of them carried the same nauseating scent.

A large wood stove was against the east wall, and hanging above it were several cast iron frying pans, "pre-greased", one might say, with either congealed leftover bacon fat or the aforementioned bear fat.

"Best to leave the door open," Peter said. "That way the bears can come in when they like, and they do less damage."

Dad must have made a rather quick appraisal, as he said, "Let's eat lunch on the table out front."

We all sat down to devour the sandwiches Mom had made for us. We enjoyed some fruit she had packed as a dessert.

With the meal over, Dad said, "You know, Peter, I think that we did so well this morning that, rather than stay and fish more this evening, maybe we should just head back right after lunch and get the boys home before dark."

I don't remember any reply from Mr. Vacon, but both Bob and I nodded vigorously in agreement with Dad's wisdom. The prospect of a five-mile walk back, making it ten miles round trip that day, held more appeal than the thought of staying in a bear-inviting camp that reeked of cooking fat and animal scat.

We made sure we had moss covering the trout in the creel and began the trek back. As we re-entered the woods, I looked back out over the meadow and Bloody Creek, and saw some black ducks flying in and settling into the small pond just in front of the cabin. It was like a Robert Bateman painting, pure magic.

Peter entertained us with more tales as we walked back, which helped the hike pass quickly. My brother and I had just experienced our best-ever fishing, and had learned to become fly fishermen. We were now members of the fraternity of brothers of the long rod. We had also learned about catch and release, about the woods and those who lived there, and the wildlife they depended on. We had heard woods tales and were richer for it. Carrying our trout actually made the walk lighter, and having Peter and his stories as an accompaniment only added to the quality of the experience.

Arriving at the Jeep, we put our gear behind the back seat, and Bob and I got in, cradling the creel between us like the prize it was. Dad quietly handed Peter the guide's fee for the contracted two days, plus a healthy tip.

"Thanks, Peter," he said. "You've given us all a true wilderness adventure. The boys will never forget this."

Dad was absolutely correct.

4: North to Nova Scotia

Figure 5: Hooper Lake

I am not quite sure how Dad managed to pull it off, but in 1970 he talked Mom into moving the family to Nova Scotia permanently. He may have enticed her with the locale, but getting her to move away from the Groton area of Massachusetts, where her family had lived for over three centuries, well, there must have been some adult discussions that I am glad I don't remember much about.

Dad was a biology professor at Tufts University in Medford and had been offered a job as head of the Biology Department at Acadia University, his alma mater, in Wolfville, Nova Scotia. I do remember that Mom and Dad discussed this potential move with us kids, and I was certainly very excited by the idea of moving full time to the province I had become so enamoured with.

We drove to Nova Scotia to tour the Acadia campus and explore the general area of Canning and Wolfville, where the bribe became apparent. We were looking at small hobby farms, with the idea that Mom and Dad would build a new house on enough land to have several horses. This, of course, immediately had my sister onside with the move.

Bob loved his school, Groton School, and would stay in residence so that he could graduate from there. I was very impressed with Acadia as a potential place to study, and the area had fishing opportunities, so I was in! In the end, Mom agreed and the big move began.

My parents bought a farmhouse with a large barn that would serve as temporary housing. Eventually they also bought forty acres of land with a small barn, where they planned to build the new house.

The move occurred that summer, and for the first time we visited the cottage that year as local residents instead of summer visitors.

My brother and I were by now keen fly fishermen, and we often joined Dad on his one-day, or even just evening, flyfishing trips. Most often, we would simply wade into the lake right in front of the cottage, which was perfectly situated for such brief adventures, and then work our way downstream, where the Annis River flowed out of the lake, past the old mill and so on.

In retrospect, the flyfishing was superb; most evenings we would catch and release a number of trout—both the native brook trout and the introduced brown trout. We didn't have to worry about catching horned pout as they seldom hit a fly and, better still, there was zero chance of hooking an eel on a fly in the slow-running water!

A typical evening would see us begin to pick up fish right in front of our uncle's cottage across the river, against the old stone wall that protruded into the stream there, or just below where our aunt and uncle had made a small dock for launching their canoes and their rowboat. The little pool between the wall and the dock was just that much deeper that larger trout would lie in wait for a fly or another morsel to be swept downstream.

Across the river, the backcast was open for the most part because, to reach this, one would have to wade halfway across the river, which was waist-deep at that point. If we made a proper cast, the fly would land softly just below the stone wall and be caught in the current, and if we used a dry fly—our favourite to use there—it would twirl gently along in the eddies.

We had to be watchful because, as the fly approached the dock, the action could begin at any moment. A trout would make a swirl at the fly, and we had to be quick to raise our rod tip to hook it, lest it just smack at the fly. Most often, if we missed the fish, it would refuse any other offerings, so we had to hope there was another fish in there, or move on.

One evening, I was fishing with a small Royal Coachman dry fly and had made a good cast. I followed intently as the fly danced along the water, heading for the inside pier of the small dock.

The water erupted as a good trout hit, and as I raised the rod tip, I could feel the weight of a nice fish.

The fish, a large brook trout, swam quickly away from me, stripping line out of my hand as he tried to get under the dock. Knowing that manoeuvre would likely snag my line on the pier piling, I pulled against the thrust of the fish and managed to turn it toward me.

The trout, not wanting to be in shallow water, headed for the deepest water in front of it, which was the lake behind me.

I was furiously winding the reel as the trout swam right past me, headed for the main outlet of the lake and open water. My little reel screamed as the trout continued stripping line out, and I thought briefly about how much line I had on the reel.

The answer was, not enough!

Still fairly new to flyfishing, I had not thought to put any backing on the reel. This meant that when the trout got to ninety feet away, the length of a fly line, the reel stopped turning and, with a solid-sounding *thunk*, three things happened almost simultaneously. First, because there was no more line to play out, the rod bent practically double. Second, not knowing enough to "bow to the fish," I simply tried to turn him by raising my tip higher (which is precisely the wrong thing to do); and third, the leader, under the pressure of a good fish and no more line, parted just above the hook.

With a *twang* the line came back toward me, and then was slack. The fish had escaped, and I had learned a lesson.

Oh, and I needed another Royal Coachman!

~

Most evenings at the cottage we would entertain ourselves with the flyfishing right at our doorstep, but occasionally we would try some other spots nearby.

A couple of years earlier, Dad had discovered a meadow a mile or so upstream from the Steer Hole. He caught some lovely trout there, and, because it was my sister's fifth birthday, he named the spot the Lisa 5 Hole. In years to come, this would be a favourite place of mine, because it was on our river (that is, simply further upstream on the Annis), which meant the same fish were available —brook and brown trout.

We would fish there by parking just before a little private bridge that led up a long farm lane to a house that overlooked the meadow. The bridge marked a good place to step into the river, which was only knee-deep in the summer in those days, and just below waist-deep after a freshet.

We'd fish downstream, which meant streamers or wet flies for the most part, and we would have to be careful, as the alders on the side of the watershed were tight to the bank, leaving little room for error.

I learned to cast carefully to avoid losing a fly in the alders, but I also learned that the alders did something else: they provided cover for the trout! I discovered the trick was to get the fly near to the bank but under the overhanging alders—a delicate thing to master—but almost instantly a young angler was rewarded if he could manage the cast, as the trout were willing.

About two hundred yards downstream, a small spring-fed brook ran into the main river, just behind a bank of alders. The colder water from this feeder stream meant there would be trout there, since trout prefer cooler water, especially in midsummer.

Approaching the Lisa 5 Hole, if we were careful, we could catch a few trout, and some might be good-sized. We saw a seventeen-inch brown trout feeding there for two years before Grampy finally hooked him and brought him in to hand.

Now that we lived in Nova Scotia, we came down to the cottage on long weekends. We explored the meadow more thoroughly, and I got to name my own spot another two hundred yards downstream. On the Victoria Day weekend, I discovered another spring hole that was on the left side of the river, at the far end of the meadow. It was just after the NHL playoffs, when the Chicago Black Hawks, led by Bobby Hull, a left-winger, had lost to the hated Montreal Canadiens in the seventh game of the NHL finals.

One of my heroes at the time, besides Bobby Orr, was Johnny Bucyk, the great Boston Bruins left-winger (everyone in my family were Bruins fans, of course). So it seemed only fitting that I name the hole for the most exciting players in the game: the Left-Winger Hole!

Besides being able to visit our Deerfield cottage more often, although for shorter periods of time, the move to Nova Scotia also meant that I could learn about flyfishing a whole new area of the province. The first year my family moved to Nova Scotia, my brother and I both stayed in Groton for the school year. Bob decided to stay on at Groton School, the famous private preparatory school, to finish out his school years. I attended Lawrence Academy, Groton's other fine private school, literally in my mother's parents' backyard.

But when the new house was being built in the heart of the Annapolis Valley the year after the move, with the enticement of all the fishing and other outdoor sports available, for my final year of high school I chose to attend the public school in Canning, Nova

Scotia. Acadia had already agreed that it was a wise choice for me if I was to attend the university, because I'd had precious little Canadian content in my schooling up to that time. Besides, Acadia said they'd accept me after grade 11 if I wished.

I wished.

~

The Annapolis Valley of Nova Scotia is known for apple orchards and extremely high tides—the highest tides measuring more than fifty vertical feet!

The Valley is formed by the rising of the main part of Nova Scotia to the south, creating the South Mountain, and the Appalachian continuance of the coastal mountain range, the North Mountain, forming the other side of the Valley, which runs roughly east/west. Wolfville, home to Acadia University, lies at the base of the South Mountain. And across the Valley, which is only ten or so miles wide, Canning lies at the base of the North Mountain.

There are towns and villages up and down the length of the Valley, although it is mostly lightly populated, being chiefly an agricultural area.

There are also two relatively large rivers. The larger, the Annapolis River, begins just south of Aylesford and runs south–west until it empties into the Annapolis Basin at Annapolis Royal and from there flows out into the Bay of Fundy. The smaller river is the Cornwallis, which has its headwaters near Berwick and flows northeast until it empties into the Minas Basin near Wolfville. Eventually the basin empties into the top end of the Bay of Fundy. It is the Minas Basin that has the highest tides on the planet.

There are also myriad small rivers and rivulets that run off the gentler slope of South Mountain or cascade down the steeper North Mountain.

Our farm was located on the banks of the Habitant River, a small brook, really, that came down the North Mountain near Sheffield Mills and then ran more gently through the Valley floor until it exited, right in front of our farm, into the Minas Basin just north of the confluence of the Cornwallis River, on the other side of the point from our place.

Naturally, the Habitant became my first trout stream to explore. What I found out quite quickly was that there were many small trout in the upper reaches of the stream, but further down, toward our farm, the run-off from the agricultural land that bordered the river on both sides meant that the Habitant was frequently a muddy red colour. That murkiness, combined with the pesticides and fertilizers that were also present, made fishing pretty well impossible for much of the year. Early in the spring, though, the narrow, shallow stream would be quite a good spot to practice flyfishing for very small brook trout.

This meant, of course, that I would have to explore further afield. The next stream over from us was a very small brook, the Canard River, which paralleled the Cornwallis and eventually joined it in the Minas Basin. The river's name is interesting: "canard" is French for "duck," and the brook was also known to the Mi'kmaw people as Apocheechumochwakade, meaning "home of the black duck." It had many of the same characteristics of the Habitant in that it flowed through much the same farmlands, which meant I'd have to keep exploring to find good fishing spots.

One outcome of visiting the Canard was that I met a retired fellow named Mr. Buckley, who ran a small fly shop located on the river. When I went in to buy some gear from him, we got to chatting about the fishing in the area. He graciously shared a lot of knowledge. He also was a fly-tier of some repute and was happy to share his techniques with me. He spoke of the seasons, of the various mayflies some of the flies imitate, while I drank it all in, and then put it into practice.

Mr. Buckley told me the best fishing in this end of the Valley was in the Cornwallis River, and that in May and June some large brown trout could be caught on a fly. He helped me tie some of the flies needed to go after them; his favourites were very small midge flies tied on a number 18 hook.

Trout flies are sized by number and a number 8 hook is about an inch long; the higher the number, the smaller the fly gets. The number 18 flies were tiny, about 1/20 of an inch! Tying the things was hard enough; how to fish them was going to be an even greater challenge.

Following Mr. Buckley's advice, I went forth one day into the Cornwallis, and did as instructed: I fished the tiny fly dry upriver, meaning I was standing in the knee-deep water and casting upstream. I had to watch carefully, or I'd lose sight of the fly, but I did manage to cast it properly, after a fashion at least.

I soon spotted a rise on my left, quite near the bank, just in front of a mass of aquatic weeds. I cast, and almost immediately a trout rose and sucked the small fly in.

The trout at first ran toward me, so I had to try to halt its run using just the pressure of my fly rod. I was a little anxious doing this, as I was aware not only of the tiny fly but also of the two-pound test leader I had to use to tie the fly on.

The trout turned down below me and put up a good fight, swimming quickly from bank to bank, looking for cover. As it began to tire, it eventually swam up past me and went back toward where I'd hooked it. This would be a problem, because if the trout got back into the weeds, I'd surely lose it.

Reacting hastily, I turned the fly rod slightly and managed to get the trout to swim toward the other, open, bank. The fish then began to swim more on the surface, and on its side, showing every sign of fatigue.

I tried to net it. Coming from behind the fish, I swooped upstream, only to hit the fish with the rim of the net, which sent it streaking upriver, toward a large overhanging alder.

Taking the chance that the leader would break, I applied pressure to the fish with my rod. Slowly, it turned. Taking more care this time to come fully under the trout, I netted it successfully.

A lovely seventeen-inch brown trout, with a number 18 hook planted firmly in its tongue.

~

Moving to the Valley also meant that we were nearer to family.

Dad's sister, with her family, and Dad's parents had all moved to Wolfville by this time. It meant I'd be able to reconnect with my cousin Don and his dad, Uncle Don.

One of the first outings Dad and I had with Uncle Don was typical of the fishing we would have in the Valley. One day, we went to a small stream that flowed off the South Mountain behind Aylesford, a remote stream that meant we parked the little four-wheel drive Subaru Dad owned then at the end of a dirt logging road and walked the mile or so uphill to a small beaver pond Uncle Don had found a couple of years earlier.

Although the day was overcast and threatened rain, it was warm for mid-May, so we all wore hip boots and light raingear. Hiking a mile in this gear meant we were all almost as wet inside as out by the time the pond was in sight!

The beaver pond was a beauty. It was in a small, almost round pond, shaded on two sides by a large stand of birch and alders and on a third side by a stand of willows. The pond had a small stream coming in at the top, a spring-fed trickle that bubbled merrily over the moss and rocks. The downhill side was open, and the feature that created the pond, a very large beaver dam, was impressive not only for its height but its width.

We walked to a spot just downhill of the dam as we approached the pond, meaning we were at eye level with the water when we were ten feet away. We could see a number of rings on the still water, and more up where the small stream flowed in.

Dad said he'd like to go up to the top, where the trout were showing in the current of the inlet, not surprising given that's where he could use his favourite Muddler Minnow to best effect. That left Uncle Don and me at the lower end of the pool.

At first, we tried fishing from below the pond, but it was hard to see exactly where our fly was landing, and we both missed hooking several fish. Dad, meanwhile, had caught and released several nice brook trout, and his success only hastened our attempts to get to where we could catch a fish more effectively.

"The casting would be easier if we stood on the beaver dam and cast into the pond," said my uncle.

As he clambered up onto the sticks, the mud-packed dam bounced a little.

"Be care—" Dad started to say.

Uncle Don stepped onto the edge of the dam, on the water side, by trying to balance on a small alder branch that was part of the structure. It bent and I heard an "oops" as Uncle Don's right foot plunged through the dam!

He was now standing awkwardly, with one foot about four feet higher than the other, with the lower foot crotch-deep in cold water, and the higher foot tangled in birch and alder choppings the beavers had used to create their masterpiece.

"Can you help?" Uncle Don asked quietly.

I managed to find secure footing on the dam, and reached out to pull my uncle up by his arms. He came out quite gracefully, and was soon sitting on the top of the dam, taking his hip-boot off and pouring out what seemed like gallons of water over the side of the dam.

"It isn't a fishing trip until someone goes in over their boots," Uncle Don said.

5: Wilderness flyfishing

Figure 6: Cloud Lake Wilderness

One of the advantages of attending Acadia University was that, as is the case with most other Canadian universities, the academic year runs from early September to late April. This means that one is free to pursue trout during May and June, the two prime fishing months for the western end of Nova Scotia.

There was the sticky point of having enough money to pay for gas to travel to the flyfishing spots, but that problem was solved in my second year, when I took a graveyard shift at the local radio station. I was on CKEN-FM radio from 10 PM to 2 AM, which meant that I had secured days free to go fishing!

Dad's May weekend trip still occurred. My Uncle Bob would come up on the Memorial Day long weekend with some of the group, and Dad and I would meet them at the cottage. After Dad, my brother Bob, and I had had such great fishing in the Quinan/Bloody Creek area, the group naturally gravitated toward that area for at least some of the fishing. The gang would travel in the two 4-wheel drive vehicles, Dad's Chevy Blazer and an old Toyota Land Cruiser that one of Uncle Bob's friends owned.

Dad's Blazer had an interesting start in our lives, as he purchased it just prior to the move from the United States to Canada. When we immigrated, we came in two cars—Mom, my brother and sister, and Bob's dog, a Newfoundland, in a station wagon; and Dad, me, and my dog in the Blazer.

We crossed on the *Bluenose* ferry, which was a six-hour ferry ride. One of our dogs—I'll admit it, my dog, a Brittany spaniel—was known to be claustrophobic. He'd been essentially given to us by a breeder friend as he was slightly taller than a show Brittany can be, but apparently he'd spent a lot of his life in small crates before coming to us. Colonel, or formally Chisholm's Colonel Seco, had a good line and was a great hunter, but he really didn't like small spaces.

Dad decided that, rather than crate Colonel for the ferry ride (probably because he'd seen the poor thing try to chew the metal cage bars to the point his gums would be bleeding), we could simply have him sit in the front seat and tie his leash loosely to the passenger-side door handle, as he was pretty good about being on a leash.

This proved to be a mistake.

The ferry company had a rule that passengers were not allowed down on the car deck once the crossing was underway. So we relaxed upstairs with Colonel safely stowed in the brand-new Blazer. As we were approaching Yarmouth Harbour and rounding the iconic Yarmouth Lighthouse, the announcement came over the PA that folks could proceed down to the car deck.

As Dad and I descended the stairs, we could hear the yipping of a dog, and as we approached the Blazer, the obvious destruction was beyond belief.

Colonel had chewed on everything he could reach, more or less the entire passenger side of the car's cabin. The dash was torn to pieces, with foam hanging out loosely. The armrest on the door, the window crank and the door trim were almost detached from the door itself. The glove compartment had a sort of scalloped effect underneath as the bite marks left a pattern of toothsome irregularity. Even the steering wheel had been chewed to the steel rim inside in the one spot he could reach, making a four-inch bare spot right through the plastic wheel casing.

I have to say, I was amazed at my father's composure. He was upset, but, fortunately for me and more so for Colonel, Dad did not follow through on the immediate solution, which would have involved tossing the "dummy, dummy, damn dog" out an open porthole of the ferry!

By the time of the trip to Coldstream, though, the Blazer was seven years old and had acquired a lot of other character marks along the way. It was a wonderful car to use for flyfishing trips.

Dad and I drove it to meet Uncle Bob's gang at the ferry this particular May weekend. From there, we drove together in to the cottages, got everyone settled, and then headed to Coldstream for the evening's fishing.

We parked the vehicles on the dirt road and followed Coldstream Brook as it ran under a small wooden bridge and went several hundred yards downstream to where it entered the main Tusket River. While this was far back in the woods, it wasn't true wilderness as we were still simply getting out of the car and then walking the river.

My uncle and I had a better idea. While the main gang was fishing down Coldstream, we decided we'd take the canoe off the top of the Blazer and paddle into one of the numerous lakes in the area. This would be more of the true wilderness experience we were craving, getting to places not fished by the more casual fisherman.

We drove the Blazer back to the main road that went out toward Meat Rock, where Peter Vacon had begun our flyfishing adventures years before. Just past Meat Rock the trail was rough, but the Blazer was up to it, and we didn't have far to travel to get to our destination, Canoe Lake.

We did have to drag the canoe, an aluminum, seventeen-foot Grumman, through some rather heavy brush, but we managed to get to the lake and launch without a problem. We paddled to the east, where on the topo maps we could see a small brook entering a cove that was in the easternmost tip of the lake.

As we rounded one of the points, we saw a pair of loons, which darted out of the way as we approached. When we began to hear running water, we knew we must be close.

The scene was beautiful.

The little brook was actually flowing over a small ledge, making a miniature waterfall as the stream entered the lake proper. Uncle Bob and I looked at each other and smiled.

There were fish rising in the foam where the brook entered and all along the lake edge where the flow made the water move. This colder running water was just what the trout wanted, as it offered easy pickings to feed on the flies and other morsels that floated downstream and were carried out into the lake.

flyfishing from a canoe isn't as easy as standing on the shore, so we landed the boat near the outflow before we began fishing. Just as at Bloody Creek, on the first cast a large fish hit my Muddler Minnow streamer and at the same time Uncle Bob had one on—a double in flyfishing parlance!

The fish were fat and filled with mayflies that they'd been gorging on, so much so that when we lifted one up, the flies actually fell out of its stuffed mouth!

Uncle Bob and I fished for a time, but soon we had to think about getting back to pick up the others. The sky had become overcast, and it was cold for May; there were actually flurries in the air as we paddled back.

With numb fingers we managed to tie the canoe back onto the

car and we headed for Coldstream. We arrived to find that their fishing had not been as good, and Dick was particularly upset because he'd felt something crawling on him after the hike down to the main river.

Upon inspection he had found about a dozen ticks on himself, many around his waist, stopped in their upward migration from his legs by the tightness of his belt. It was apparently quite the scene as he stripped quickly to check for any other transgressing insects.

For the rest of us, tick checks were nothing new. Early in the 1900s, or so the story goes, ticks were introduced to Nova Scotia from the United States by hitching a ride on hunting dogs coming here with upland bird hunters. Nova Scotia is known for its woodcock hunting and people from all over the States would come here in the 1930s and 1940s to hunt for the migratory upland birds. The ticks have been here ever since, and are simply regarded as an annoyance and part of the outdoors life in the summer.

That perception has changed, I would note, with the finding in the early 2000s that Lyme-carrying ticks are now here as well—an unwelcome development requiring much more care.

~

Two of my closest friends in university and I also took advantage of the fact that my family's cottage in Deerfield was only two hours from campus. We made several trips down to Deerfield and fished more remote areas, since we all loved to explore.

One year, Chris, Wayne, and I had already had some excellent flyfishing near Wolfville on the opening weekend in April, when we'd simply driven one of the back roads nearby to get to East Dalhousie. Wayne was an experienced fly fisherman, and we took Chris under our wing and taught him the mechanics and even got him into some fly-tying.

We would take a car, normally Dad's four-wheel drive, to reach the headwaters of the LaHave River. Wayne had caught a slink salmon here, meaning an Atlantic salmon that had come in to breed the previous fall, had overwintered, and was heading back downstream.

We discovered some beautiful backwoods flyfishing could be had. At one place, we found a spot that required a good mile-long hike to get to the outflow of a lake into the LaHave system. We were into an area that would not normally be fished by others, given that the fishing was good enough for many nearer the roads.

Arriving at the lake in East Dalhousie one afternoon, we found the trout willing, and Chris was getting very good at casting his homemade fly to the eager fish. We caught and released a number of fish, but for a time the flyfishing slowed.

Wayne, who liked to brag about his prowess as a fly fisherman, caught a couple more small trout, and then, in an ill-advised attempt to get further out into the lake, he stepped over a sunken log right into a hole and went over his chest waders. Now we had a fishing trip.

Fortunately, he had a belt tied around his waist on the outside, preventing the water rushing in and pulling him under!

Chris added to Wayne's woes when he caught a nine-inch trout and then winked at me. "Wayne," he said, "I'll bet I catch the next trout!"

"You're on," our soggy companion shouted back without looking in our direction. "I've got a bunch rising out here."

Chris had gently let the fish back into the water, without Wayne noticing. After maybe ten seconds, he started talking to the trout, "Here fishy, fishy..." As he pulled up his rod tip he said, "Wow, got a pretty good one here!"

Only Wayne was surprised.

Wayne eventually forgave Chris once the ploy was revealed, and later that year the three of us decided to go to Deerfield for the Easter weekend. Easter was a bit late that year, a mid-April event, which meant that it was quite cool as we entered the cottage.

The unheated building had one heat source, a huge open fireplace in the living room. Normally, we'd have slept in the adjoining bedrooms off the main living space, but this weekend was so cold that Chris decided he'd rather sleep on the couch. He pulled it near the fireplace for greater warmth. I thought his idea wise, so I put the two big armchairs together adjacent to the couch.

Wayne declared he'd sleep on the daybed, just on the other side of the armchairs, with his beagle, Snoopy, who'd come for the weekend.

The arrangement worked well, although both Chris and I noticed, as we stoked the fire that night, that Snoopy wasn't anywhere in sight; he'd actually crawled into the sleeping bag with Wayne and had buried himself inside the warm covering. Maybe it was colder than we had thought.

The next morning, we set out on our wilderness trek. We had decided to explore the main Tusket River above a fishing hole the family calls The Hedge. This part of the Tusket is quite remote, but The Hedge is accessible from a nearby dirt road.

A couple of Dad's gang had the year before put a canoe in at another family fishing spot, Big Meadow, and had canoed downstream to The Hedge. They reported good fishing and had seen a "small pocket" of what looked like flowing water about halfway down, so two miles or so upstream from The Hedge.

Chris, Wayne, and I deduced from a topographic map that the flowing water coming into the main Tusket would have to be a brook coming out of one of the lakes nearby. We packed a lunch and drove to The Hedge, where we parked and began walking upriver.

The walking was not easy. We hugged the river as best we could, but there were two swamps we had to traverse, and there was no path. The river on the way up looked very fishy in places, as there were riffled runs and deep pools, but our plan was to walk up to where the brook entered and then fish downstream back to the beginning.

Along the way, we saw a deer on the other side of the river, in what is now part of the Tobeatic Wilderness, and we saw many ducks flying up and down the river. The day had turned warmer and was partly overcast, with a slight breeze and a touch of warmth to the south wind.

We arrived at the pocket and were immediately rewarded for

our hike. There, as we looked down on the pool from a small rise just downstream, was the brook forming a line of foam as it entered the main river, which was perhaps 150 feet wide at this point—a very wide expanse for the Tusket. We could see trout rising in the pool right under where we stood, and all the way up-river to the opening where the brook came in. The water was dimpling for about 100 yards, on both sides of the river—covering the entire pool really—and we could see several nice fish among the rises.

Hurriedly, we assembled our fly rods. Wayne and I had chest waders in a pack, and so he suggested he would go out to the far side, while Chris and I fished the brook where it enters. His idea was sound, as this meant Chris, in his hip boots, would be the nearest to shore, while Wayne and I could wade farther out. This way, all three of us could fish at once in the broad pool.

I took Chris to the brook and we could see trout taking flies below the surface, just behind the bank where the brook flowed out. "There," I said, pointing. "Wade out just above the brook next to the bank here, and fish downstream to the rises and into the brook's mouth."

Chris did precisely as instructed and immediately went three inches deeper than his hip boots. Once again, we had a fishing trip!

Ignoring the cold water in his boots, he waded carefully to about thirty feet upstream from the brook's mouth. A perfect first cast put his hand-tied Wooly Bugger into the flow, and immediately a trout hit. Chris set the hook and was into a very nice fish.

The trout obligingly swam almost directly out into the middle of the river, away from the brook's mouth, which gave Chris deeper water to work with and away from where other trout were still rising. Chris managed to get the fly line onto his reel and played the trout that way back and forth for a few moments, until the fish would make a run and Chris, quite skilfully for a novice, let the line zip out.

The main river had no real snags in it, so Chris simply stood there and fought the fish as it was upstream from him. As the trout tired, it started to come back downstream toward him.

"Would you like some help?" I said, doing my best Peter Vacon impersonation.

"Sure," said Chris.

The trout was already on its side as it came down almost to Chris. I simply put my small, single-handed trout net out into the flow and the fish essentially swam right into the net.

A thirteen-inch brook trout—Chris's first really big fish.

Wayne, meanwhile, had caught and released several nice fish, and after setting Chris up, I also got in on the action.

We had lunch eventually and stood admiring the pool, which was quieter now, but all three of us saw the rises at the tail end, downstream.

We fished downriver after lunch, and caught and released dozens of brook trout of varying sizes. We each kept a couple of fish, including Chris's first trout, so that we could have a traditional brook trout breakfast the next morning before heading back to Wolfville.

Chris and Wayne agreed: the Billy Hole became part of our lexicon.

~

At the end of my final year at university, when I was studying for a Bachelor of Education, a plan for a really big wilderness trip was hatched for the weekend before the Victoria Day weekend. A friend of my father's, Henry, was looking for three people to join him on a trip to a very remote part of Nova Scotia along the Eastern Shore, near Liscomb.

Henry's friend Roger had already agreed to go, and the two of them were going to take another friend of theirs, Bruce. They needed someone else to help Bruce man his canoe. When they approached me, I said yes instantly.

We drove in Henry's four-wheel-drive Toyota from Wolfville to Halifax and then headed up Highway 7 toward Liscomb and Guysborough County. We turned off Highway 7 and drove another hour or so up a very narrow dirt road, until we came to the landing where we'd launch the canoes.

The area we would be fishing is now a provincially-designated wilderness area, but in those days it was simply remote.

We launched the canoes, loaded with our gear, and paddled across the lake to reach a small camp a friend of Henry's had given us permission to use. Once we were settled at the camp, we started a fire to take off the chill, but when we saw fish rising in the main lake, Bruce and I paddled our canoe toward some rises and caught some trout for breakfast.

After we returned to the camp, everyone settled in for a good night's sleep, knowing that the next night would be in a tent.

Early the next morning, we got the fire going again and enjoyed the trout with some bacon for breakfast. The May sun was strong but there was a little breeze, which was good because we had noted on the paddle the evening before the blackflies had already started.

After breakfast, we got our gear together, carefully wrapping sleeping bags and clothes in garbage bags in case of an unplanned dunking, and off we set to go downriver about ten miles.

The planned route had three portages, two long ones of maybe a quarter mile and a shorter one of maybe two hundred yards in the middle. I was used to portaging a canoe, so on the way down, I did both the longer carries, while Bruce lugged our gear.

Bruce's canoe was heavier than mine: his was a sixteen-foot aluminum boat, whereas mine was a wood and canvas craft. Aluminum is sturdier for banging against the rocks we knew we'd encounter, so that's what we went with.

I tied the paddles into the thwarts to make a yoke and carried the canoe without a problem. We reached the end of the third portage about lunchtime and saw fish rising in the river spreading out before us.

"We're not fishing here yet," said Henry, as Bruce started to pull out a fly rod. "We'll get to the last still water where we'll camp, and then we'll fish."

Bruce shot a look toward Henry, but put the fly rod back in his pack.

As Bruce and I paddled our canoe, following Roger and Henry in theirs, we could see trout dimpling the surface all around us. The still water was full of rising fish, and we could see mayflies sitting on the water and being sucked down.

A mayfly hatch was occurring, a sight that sets a trout fisher's pulse racing, as it means the fish will hit your fly willingly of you can match the fly on the water with your artificial one.

We kept paddling as Henry urged us on just a bit further. Bruce harrumphed quietly.

We finally reached a point where the still water entered a larger lake and then constricted into a narrower stream, just above another still water.

"Here's where we camp," said Henry. "Let's fish just down through the still water and then come back and set up camp."

It turned out that Henry was absolutely correct to not fish on the way down, as we'd have never gotten so far, for the moment we began fishing we were into trout. All sizes of brook trout were hitting the flies rather recklessly. It didn't really seem to matter what fly we had on, they were hungry fish!

We caught several for breakfast and released over thirty fish each in the two hours or so of fishing we had there, before Henry decided we ought to set up camp for the night.

We got the two tents up quickly and made a small fire for supper. Henry and Roger had brought along some stew, and Bruce and I had brought canned corned beef hash. We shared some wonderful homemade bread that Roger's wife had sent. We boiled some water for coffee and spent the evening in quiet contentment.

The loons called to each other during the night, the blackflies mercifully were kept at bay by a breeze that had come up, and we all enjoyed a great night's sleep dreaming of the flyfishing we'd just had and of more to come.

In the morning, while we feasted on trout and bacon, Henry divulged that we would all paddle to the end of the still water, from which he and Roger would go up a small brook. Bruce and I were to wait while they explored the lake at the top of the small stream.

This sounded like an excellent plan, since we really only had a couple of hours if we were to get back to the camp before dark.

Paddling through the still water below our campsite, we saw a family of beavers. The male slapped his tail furiously on the water as we paddled past, warning the rest of us invaders. Ducks flew overhead with their wings making a soft *swishing*, and a family of mergansers skittled quickly across the surface just above the mouth of Henry's stream, their movement creating small v-wakes as they went along.

Roger and Henry pulled their canoe up into a marshy spot. The river made a rustling sound as it passed, and as Henry stepped out of the canoe, his boots sunk deep into the soft mud. The lily pads shifted as the canoe was pushed toward shore, and a bullfrog leaped off of one, after croaking loudly at being disturbed.

"We'll be back in an hour or so," Henry said. "You guys fish here, and we'll meet you and start heading for camp after we explore the lake above."

Bruce and I turned our canoe around and paddled back a couple of hundred yards to where we'd seen some fish rising in a small side pool. Compared to yesterday, the fishing was slower, but there were fish to be seen. I think because they were stuffed from yesterday's hatch of mayflies, the trout this day were much harder to fool.

After about a half hour, Bruce said, "Why don't we paddle to the end of the still water and fish where we heard the running water?" I eagerly agreed and we paddled downstream.

The river turned from a fairly deep still water to a body of rushing water just at the end of the pool. We could see the rocks and hear the falls long before we got there, so we had lots of time to estimate a proper place to beach our canoe and walk to the top of the rapids.

Neither of us were wearing waders or boots since it was quite a dangerous thing to do while paddling a canoe, so this was "wading wet." But the day had warmed up, it was sunny with only a few clouds, so neither of us minded the dampness of our sneakers.

I cast a Royal Coachman dry fly into the top pool just below a large rock, and directly into the fast current. I felt a tap against the fly and pulled, but missed the fish. I cast again and this time the trout hit more solidly; I was into a very big one.

Figure 7: A Royal Coachman

The fish at first started to go downstream, but there were some large rocks just below that would have meant it'd have to swim right against the shore to get past. To my good fortune, the fish simply turned and, as the trout had done before, ran right past me and out toward the still water's depths. Having learned from my earlier experiences, I had backing on my reel, which proved a good thing because the trout quickly had my full line out, and was into the backing.

The reel screamed while the fish ran, but it didn't break the leader this time as I started winding back and worked the fish with the rod. Bruce was slack-jawed. He'd never seen a really big trout, and this was new to him.

I fought the trout in the open water, thank heavens, for probably four or five minutes before it began to tire. I had my small trout net ready, and as the fish was coming back downstream, I resisted the urge to coax it to swim into the net, which would have scared it into another run, and instead came from behind the fish and lifted up. The trout was eighteen inches, with beautiful markings and a silver sheen to its side.

"A sea trout!" I exclaimed.

Bruce asked what I meant. I explained that, just like Atlantic salmon, some brook trout are born in the freshwater, then run out into saltwater briefly and return upstream to breed. This makes the trout much larger and also turns their flesh to a fiery orange. They also are the nicest tasting trout, in my opinion.

In the hour or so that we fished afterwards, we caught and released dozens of nice trout, many sea trout and also some native brook trout. Bruce kept one of his biggest fish, a fat fifteen-inch sea trout. We were having great fun.

"Hey," we heard from the woods. "What are you guys up to?"

It was Henry and Roger returning from their adventure. They had gone all the way upstream, found the lake, but had seen not a single fish until they got back to the still water.

"Sea trout," said Bruce.

"*Really*!" Henry said. "Man..."

Before we headed back, Roger and Henry did get a chance to catch some of the sea trout, and we all enjoyed picking up some native brook trout during the paddle back.

We had one small mishap that is recorded in the camp's diary.

Bruce somehow managed on the way back to talk me into both of the long portages again, though I can't quite recall how. In any case, on the shortest portage, he was transporting the canoe as I'd shown him, using the paddles for a yoke and carrying the boat on his shoulders. Henry and Roger were in front of us. I followed behind them, carrying the packs and walking in front of Bruce.

I heard an *oomph* from behind me that made me turn to see the canoe lying upside down on the ground, just as Bruce had been carrying it, but with no sign of Bruce! A muffled call for help emanated from beneath the boat.

Putting the packs down, I ran to the canoe and lifted the bow off the ground. Bruce was waist-deep in a beaver hole, with the canoe pinning him to the ground.

Bruce looked scared, but we handily pulled him out of the hole; however, I'm sure he didn't appreciate our laughter.

"Now we have a fishing trip," I said.

In the camp diary, we dutifully noted the events of our weekend. We couldn't resist including the advice that, if one saw a canoe upside down on the side of the trail, it might be best to lift it up and let Bruce out.

All of us had caught and released over a hundred trout each that weekend. I had caught a couple of fish on the way back to the camp that I would bring home to Mom and Dad, as did Bruce and Henry and Roger. Our flyfishing and conservation effort was clear; none of us even thought about taking close to the quota we were each allowed per day, with a fifteen-trout possession limit per person.

An article that appeared in the newspaper a couple of weeks later, after the Victoria Day weekend, reported that several anglers were caught in that general vicinity in possession of over one hundred trout each. That kind of greed has to be squashed by all anglers who want to pass on such great experiences to future generations.

I have photographs and a description of the weekend in my personal journal. To me, it's much better to fill our memories than our creels.

6: The Hedge

Figure 8: The Hedge

flyfishing is about being outdoors as much as it is about going after the fish. When I was a kid, Dad and some of the family would drive the forty-five minutes from the cottage to the woods of Kempt, Nova Scotia, where we'd go past the fire tower and down a long dirt road that ended near the Sunday Lake bridge over the Tusket River.

The Hedge was a backwater pool, just off the main river, that had a blueberry field overlooking it and a gently sloped bank down to the water. I always enjoyed these outings because it meant that family could come along while we went fishing.

I have a photo in my study of my grandfather, Dad, and a great-uncle all fishing The Hedge in the 1940s, a colourized image that captures the spirit of the place quite beautifully. Dad is out near the main pool, on the big rock flyfishing. Grampy, in his trademark floppy white hat, is at the main hole, with a night crawler on, no doubt. And Uncle Will, in a suit coat and tie and formal hat, is standing on the edge of the inner pool of The Hedge getting his gear ready before making a first cast. This leads me to think it may have been an after-church kind of fishing day, as Dad and Grampy would always have fishing gear and a change of clothes ready in the car, whereas Uncle Will may not have thought of that.

The picture is typical of our trips to The Hedge, though, in that family members joined us.

My earliest memories of the spot include one of the few times I can remember going fishing with my grandmother and my great-aunt Mattie. My grandparents were very special to me, and had an interesting history that shaped them both into the people all who knew them loved.

At age eighteen, my grandfather, like many men in Yarmouth County and, indeed, like many men across Canada, joined the Canadian Armed Forces to fight in the First World War. Grampy saw action at Vimy Ridge and at Passchendaele.

During the Battle of Passchendaele, Grampy's unit was hunkered down in trenches across a field from the opposing force, when a mortar round was lobbed in the direction of the Canadian troops, and the trench caved in. My grandfather was buried by the collapsing earth, and only because his riding crop was sticking out above the ground could his comrades tell where he was. They dug him out, injured but alive.

Grampy was transported first to Belgium and then to France, before winding up in a hospital just outside London, England, where he spent the rest of the war recuperating.

In 1918, he was well enough to go home but, upon arrival in Halifax, he discovered that, while he had been travelling across the Atlantic, his father had died at home in Port Maitland. Grampy also learned on a phone call home that his mother had plans to go live with some family members who had moved to Massachusetts. He declared that he'd return to England and find that "pretty girl who served him soup in the hospital."

He did just that.

In what must have been a whirlwind of activity, Emerson Ladd Curry married Gertrude Lily Alice Montgomery in a small church in Peckham, England. Within a month they were heading across the Atlantic, and eventually to Grampy's home in Port Maitland.

My grandmother was very special to me, as grandmothers tend to be to their grandchildren, but her story is also noteworthy. She was a war bride who had never been much further than the outskirts of London, yet she decided to follow her heart and marry a man who would move her to a foreign land she'd never seen. Her letters back home show she was homesick, but that she also appreciated the life she had here in Canada.

Great-Aunt Mattie, Grampy's only full sister, was an equally interesting lady. She had become a schoolteacher. About the same time Grampy went overseas, she did as well. Her service was for her church, and she became a missionary in India.

After the war, Mattie and my grandmother became close friends during the visits home that Mattie would make. They would walk on the beach in Port Maitland, and Mattie would comfort Grandmother, who was thinking of England and family across the water.

Mattie would send us kids trinkets from India, things like stamps with exotic colours and patterns, and little hand-carved elephants. We always looked forward to when Aunt Mattie would come home.

The day we travelled to The Hedge with Grammy and Aunt Mattie in the back of the car with Grampy, Dad and me up front; I was about age seven. We took a picnic lunch. As we "men" went to fish The Hedge, the ladies placed a blanket to sit on and began picking blueberries.

Dad and Grampy took me out to the main pool, trying to prevent me from stepping off the boggy trail, for the bank of The Hedge's main pool is really a kind of floating bog. Of course, I did step off the trail, making it a fishing trip right away, and was rescued from a deeper watery misstep only because Dad had a tight grip on my hand and pulled me back.

"Be careful," he said. "If you make too much commotion you'll scare the fish!" Less about survival, more about the trout!

We set up almost identically to the picture in my study: Dad got me situated on the main pool on the grassy bank, and then he waded out to the big rock, and Grampy helped me bait the hook and cast my bobber and night crawler out into the main hole. He then walked the short distance across the boggy tundra and proceeded to do the same, night crawler and bobber, in the inner hole.

The Hedge is interesting geographically as it has a spring hole at one end, and it opens out into the main Tusket River at the other end. This means there are the three spots to fish, which is great for a family trip.

My bobber soon began the now-familiar dance, and I hooked a nice trout in short order. Grampy appeared beside me and swooped the fish with his long-handled dip net. At the same time, Dad was catching some fish out around the rock at the other end of the pool with his fly rod, and I remember thinking how graceful his casting was.

Grampy decided to abandon the inner hole and fished beside me for the rest of our visit this day. We both caught several lively brook trout, and did keep some in Grampy's old creel, placing them carefully on the moss we gathered from the bank. A familiar, yet memorable trip.

Once the trout stopped biting so readily, Grampy suggested we take the bobbers off and fish deeper. This was a bit trickier as it meant we'd cast our worms out and then let them sink to the bottom, and after letting them sit for a few moments, we'd retrieve them slowly back toward us.

Grampy was a master at doing this. He could sense when the night crawler was going over a log and when there was a fish interested in the bait. It was harder fishing for me, but I eventually learned to do the same thing. We both caught a few more trout, and a bit bigger this time.

The fishing ended when I hooked a large eel—it had swallowed the hook way down its throat. Grampy had to use his small pocket knife that he always carried to pry open the eel's mouth and then cut around a bit to get the hook out. It is this incident that causes me to this day to use a Swiss Army knife as a keychain, a small, family-based homage to my grandfather.

The eel was injured but still lively. He released it back into the water. "Don't tell your grandmother," he said.

When we got back up the little hill at the top of the bank, Grammy and Aunt Mattie had picked several quarts of blueberries.

"I think we'll make a blueberry grunt," said Grammy, referring to the family's favourite dish of blueberries cooked in a pan with small dumplings of dough, and all covered with blueberry sauce—a dessert that was just as delightful as the day.

We all sat on the blanket to eat our lunch of sandwiches and fruit, and just watched the river as it meandered along in front of us. Being outdoors with family was, and still is, a cherished time.

~

After I learned to fly-fish, The Hedge presented even more interesting fishing. As a teen, I'd wade across the bog to the far side, the way Dad would, and fish the rock near where the main river curved by the opening to The Hedge itself.

The stand there for flyfishing was perfect: open both in the front and the back, meaning there was little to concern yourself with on either the forward cast or the backcast, except for finding the fish. We did have to be careful casting, in that the trout would spook easily, because this was not running water but a still water.

We'd simply have to pick our day—a gentle breeze and slightly overcast, especially right after a rainstorm in July or August, was the day to go to The Hedge.

The Hedge became the first place I learned to fly-fish with a dry fly. With a streamer or a wet fly, you are flyfishing using the current to "swim" your fly to where the fish will take it. You can also cast a wet fly in a still water like The Hedge and your retrieve causes the fly to have enough action to fool the fish into hitting the lure.

But sometimes the trout zone in on hatching insects. On those days, you have to figure out what the fish are eating, because they simply won't look at much else in the way of flies.

This is when my grandfather would switch away from flies and use a worm, but when I became a fly fisherman, I simply found it more fun, if less effective, to try to "match the hatch" and figure out what fly to use to fool the trout into striking.

With a dry fly, you cast the fly that has lots of hackle on it to make it sit on top of the water, aiming toward where you see a rising trout, and then twitch the fly gently by working the line and the rod tip. Dry flyfishing is exciting because you actually see the trout hit the fly, but with brook trout you have to be quick to raise your tip when they hit the dry fly; if you are too slow, the trout simply spit the fly out before you can hook them. You develop a reflex for this, but it does take practice.

There's a thrill, though, in making a nice cast, with the fly landing softly on the water's surface, followed by the water surging as the trout comes up to suck the fly in, and then the rush as the fish turns and you raise your tip to set the hook in the fish's mouth.

And a fly rod is so much more fun than a bait rod to play a trout once it's hooked like this, because the fly rod itself is more flexible and thus you can feel the fish more than with a bait rod. Even modern ultra-light spin fishing outfits, as fun as they are to use, to me are not equal to the experience of a fly rod and flyfishing.

One year, my uncle Bob and I were fishing The Hedge on the annual trip of Dad's former gang, and now Uncle Bob's, coming up to Nova Scotia on the May weekend. Uncle Bob and I had dropped the four men of his group up at Big Meadow Brook, a tributary of the Tusket River about four miles upstream from The Hedge. The group, my dad and three others, had two canoes and the plan was for them to canoe down Big Meadow Brook to the Tusket and then fish down to The Hedge, where Uncle Bob and I would be waiting with the transportation.

Uncle Bob and I drove the vehicles, he in his Toyota, me in our family pickup truck, down to The Hedge, where we parked and waited. We waded out to The Hedge pool, and did not see a single trout rising. We weren't long determining The Hedge simply wasn't going to pay off for us on this day.

We realized that we were going to be waiting a couple of hours. I don't remember who had the idea, but one of us looked at the topographic map.

Uncle Bob said, "You know, I've never fished the lake across the road in behind here. It's only a mile and a half, maybe we should go try!"

Now, for me to undertake following my uncle's advice on any map-related trip into the woods is not something I would normally do lightly. Precedent is the reason for what can only be deemed prudent hesitation.

When I was about seven, so my brother, Bob, would have been five, Uncle Bob told us of a fun thing we could do one evening: a snipe hunt. As he explained it, he would take us into the little woodlot behind our summer cottage, and we'd be able to sit there with bread crumbs and pillowcases. The crumbs would attract the snipe, and we'd bag them. What fun!

The hunt did not turn out quite the way our uncle envisioned, I'm certain. My mother, a bit of a practical joker herself, heard of the plan to take her young offspring on this hunt—two kids stranded in the woods in gathering darkness, no doubt getting scared stiff. What fun, indeed. Perhaps out of self-preservation with the knowledge that she'd be the one dealing with the aftermath, she let us in on the inevitable outcome. Under her guidance, we simply added a bit of a twist to the hunt.

Uncle Bob led the two of us, pillowcases and flashlights in hand, out into the woodlot. His instructions were to sit still, spread the crumbs around, and then use the flashlight to illuminate the crumb pile, and, when a snipe came to get the food, pop the bird into the sack!

He left us, and went back to the cottage, chuckling softly to himself. However, he didn't get very far when he heard two screams!

"We got one, we got one," Bob and I yelled.

Uncle Bob hurried back to us and what he saw must have been a bit of a shock. There in the clearing was a pile of feathers among the bread crumbs.

"We had one almost in the bag," Bob and I reported, "but at the last minute, it ran out and got away!"

Our uncle trudged back to the cottage with us skipping along gleefully behind. He did not understand what had happened until, upon climbing the porch stairs to the cottage, he caught sight of Mom, who was doubled over and in tears, she was laughing so hard.

Nevertheless, I put the memory of the snipe hunt aside, and I agreed to the latest adventure Uncle Bob had proposed. We even found a small path directly across the road from where we had parked.

We left a note on the windshield of the truck to explain our plan, just in case, and off we went. Although the woods were quite thick, the hike in was easy because the path was well-worn. It didn't take us long to find the lake.

There in front of us was a small body of water with a large beaver dam at the far end. We could see trout rising and gulping flies, which we could discern instantly were Hendrickson mayflies.

We both tied on dry flies—Uncle Bob tied on a Red Quill fly, and I used a Light Hendrickson, both being imitation flies for a real Hendrickson. The cast would be tricky, as the woods went right down to the pond, leaving little to no room for a backcast from the shore.

I stepped gently into the water and found that the steep bank indicated a deeper pool than we might have suspected. In any case, we had a fishing trip when my hip boots submerged four inches lower in the water than the top of my boots. Uncle Bob also waded into the water, but he went only two inches over his boots.

"Wow," he exclaimed, "that's cold water!"

The trout continued to rise around us though. I spotted a nice fish rising about thirty feet to my left and out from shore about forty feet, and Uncle Bob saw some in the other direction. Our only concern was to not hook each other on the backcast.

After several attempts, my dry fly landed nicely on the water about two feet beyond where I'd seen the fish, and almost immediately there was a large swirl and a hit. I raised the rod tip right away and the fish pulled hard. I tried to get some slack line in as rapidly as I could, but the fish was pulling so quickly that I ended up fighting it by holding the line because I couldn't wind the line in fast enough to get to play the fish from my fly reel.

The trout was in deep water and swam quickly in large circles. Eventually it tired and I could try to get it in close enough to net.

Even though I was coming from behind the fish, it must have seen the net in its struggles; as I came forward with the handle, the trout shot out into the lake another ten or fifteen feet in a split second.

Somehow, the hook didn't come out. The fish was still on and, after a bit more of a tussle, I got the fish tired out and managed to net it while still standing about ten feet offshore.

I had landed a brook trout about 16.5 inches, a beauty with a full, fat belly indicative of the huge hatch of mayflies it was feeding on. Because we were with a group of men we knew would love a trout breakfast, I kept that fish.

Uncle Bob and I did something we didn't do often: we kept a limit of five trout each.

We hiked back through the woods after an hour or so, and reached The Hedge just in time to see the two canoes appearing at the top of the river opening, heading toward the little landing in the inner pool.

They had had a fishing trip as well; Dad and Dick had flipped their canoe on a rock below the Billy Hole! When they got ashore, the group admitted they also had a pretty slow day, although the paddling had been fun. They asked if we got anything at The Hedge.

Uncle Bob said, "No, not much here. But we fished a new lake and found these."

He opened the creel and showed off ten beautiful brook trout— all around thirteen or fourteen inches, with the three largest fish each almost as big as the 16.5-incher I'd caught.

"Where *is* this lake?" Dad asked.

~

My brother Bob now teaches at Villanova University in Philadelphia, so he doesn't get as much time in Nova Scotia as he'd like. But when he and his family vacation here in the summer, we try to go flyfishing together.

On this occasion, we'd chosen The Hedge as our target. There was a slight south breeze, it was lightly overcast, and it had rained a couple of days earlier; it should have been the ideal day for flyfishing The Hedge. Being a flyfishing purist does, however, lead to surprising situations.

As we were setting up the rods, we could see trout rising in the opening to The Hedge, where it connects with the main Tusket River. Dad got down the little bank and started for the big rock, Bob headed for the main pool, and I decided to try the inner pool.

We could all see trout, but could not get anything to hit our flies. We also could not see any flies on the water, so it became a bit of a guess as to what the fish were taking. It was mid-July, so the flies should have been Stone flies, which my favourite Muddler Minnow matches, or maybe Tricos, small black or white dry flies.

I had on a Muddler Minnow, but still could not get a hit. Bob had started with a wet fly, an Alexandria, but had switched to a Trico thinking we could get some good dry flyfishing.

Nothing would take.

For a frustrating hour or so we fished The Hedge, but none of us could get a strike. Bob and I, because we were on the main and inner pools, spotted a number of larger rises out in the main river, outside The Hedge opening. We'd never fished out there wading (I had gone over it in a canoe, but had never really fished the spot that way, either).

Bob said, "Let's try the main river and see if we can catch some of those out there."

I agreed. Dad, being older and wiser, demurred and said, "I'll watch."

Figure 9: A Muddler

Bob and I both had chest waders on, so we felt we could wade out into the main river and easily get within casting distance of the rises we had seen. Neither of us could see any flies on the water, so I stuck with my Muddler and Bob said he'd simply keep the Trico on.

I waded out past the mouth of The Hedge. The bottom was soft and boggy, like the bank of The Hedge itself, not hard and gravelly like the bottom near the inner pool. In hindsight, that should have tipped me off.

As I waded out, concentrating on a small island in the main river just downstream of The Hedge, I could see many fish rising. This is why I was concentrating on where I was going and not really thinking about where I'd been. Bob was wading out behind me.

I heard a soft splash and a sound like a large gulp.

Turning around, I saw Bob's hat floating on the surface of the water, but nothing else of Bob was in view. In a moment, the water erupted as he came back to the surface. Bob had stepped in a deep hole, one that the bog two feet below covered over.

Fortunately, it was not a wide hole, and he had simply stepped back out so that his head and shoulders were now above water. The top half of his waders had filled with water, the bottom half re-ceiving only a trickle because both Bob and I waded with belts fastened tightly around our waists for just such mishaps.

"Are you okay?" shouted Dad.

Bob spluttered something unintelligible.

We fished the river anyway, as the fish were still rising and it was warm, but we could get nothing to hit our flies. I tried a variety of flies, and even used some flies I rarely use. In the end, none of us got any fish to take. We came ashore and admitted we'd been "skunked."

Flyfishing is sometimes like that, and as the saying goes, "That's why it's called fly-*fishing*, not *catching*."

There would be eggs for breakfast.

7: Big Meadow Brook

Figure 10: Big Meadow Brook

Big Meadow Brook epitomizes the history of trout fishing in the southwestern end of Nova Scotia. Of all the places I fly-fish, one of the most special is Big Meadow Brook.

There are a number of reasons for this, from the fact that my great-grandfather fished here and at least four generations of my extended family guided out of here, to the fact that the place holds so many memories. It has undergone numerous changes and has emerged as a designated Special Trout Management Zone, only to be threatened once again.

My first trip to Big Meadow Brook that I can remember was a typical one with my Grampy and my Dad in mid-July during our summer vacation to Nova Scotia. The day was warm and slightly overcast. We drove to Kempt, passing the road by the fire tower that leads to The Hedge, and crossed over the brook as we drove on what is now Highway 203 and paved, but was simply a dirt road in my youth.

Big Meadow Brook goes under the road and flows down another mile or so to meet the main Tusket River, perhaps four miles up-stream from The Hedge. Above the highway bridge, the stream is rocky and shallow for about two hundred yards, which forms the lower pool; but above this, Big Meadow Brook is a still water with only a few narrow runs and no real fast water for its entire length up to Duck Pond Brook, which enters about two miles above the bridge.

Above Duck Pond Brook, the stream becomes a very small brook that drains out of a meadow and is fed by springs and the run-off from Ikes Ridge, a small rise of land at the head of the stream. This topography makes the place a wonderful spot to canoe or kayak for almost its entire length. The long, slow, deep water draining the peat bogs below the ridge has that signature tea-colour, tannin-stained character.

Grampy, Dad, and I chose to drive up the logging road in the four-wheel-drive Jeep and park near the bottom of the still water, just above where the watershed passes through woods and then tumbles down to the lower pool above the bridge.

Walking through the boggy marsh that borders this section of the stream, we could see many pitcher plants, a medium-sized flower that has a single stalk headed with a large, deep-red bulb. A member of the carnivorous plant family, the pitcher plant traps a small amount of water in the bulb, which also has tiny hair-like barbs on the interior of the flower. When a fly or other insect comes to get a drink, they slip inside the bulb and land in the water, and can't crawl out because of the hairs. The liquid contains an enzyme that slowly dissolves and feeds on the drowned insect.

The walk across the marsh was brief, and we took a well-worn path along the riverbank. When we came to the edge of the stream, where the grass was high enough that a six-year-old needed some assistance, Grampy stomped down some of the taller grasses to create an opening I could see from.

Dad took up a position nearby with his fly rod. Grampy and I assembled our spinning rods and baited our hooks with night crawlers.

"Be careful," I heard my grandfather say. "The water is very deep."

He was correct. While the stream is not very broad, maybe seventy feet across, the bank is undercut and the stream is more than six feet deep at the spot we were fishing.

Grampy told me stories of having been here when he was my age with his father, which must have been an all-day trip from Port Maitland in those days.

Dad rose a small trout on his Parmachene Belle dry fly, and on a subsequent cast he hooked the trout. Soon afterwards, Grampy and I each had fish on, the first time we had a triple: three people having fish on at the same time.

Of course, a six-year-old with a trout on, standing next to his grampy, meant that care on the part of the elder was required to avoid a huge tangle!

We managed to land all three fish. Dad caught and released a six-inch brook trout, while I had hooked a nice eight-inch fish, and Grampy had a ten-inch beauty.

My trout was hooked lightly, and Dad suggested we release it.

I held the fish gently in my wet hands (having been told numerous times to not handle fish with dry hands to avoid stripping the protective mucous-like covering that helps a trout ward off infections) to study it. The lovely spots glistened in the subdued sunlight, and the fish wriggled slightly, which made the colours dance. Leaning over the water, I dropped the trout softly back into the water and watched it swim away.

Grampy had dispatched his trout already and had placed it in the creel with some moss. "You can have that one for breakfast," he told me.

"Thanks, but I want to catch my own," I said. I didn't realize then that Grampy was smiling at the attitude of a six-year-old, full of confidence and independence, and something that occurs infrequently, he would tell me later.

~

When I became a fly fisherman, I loved to fish at Big Meadow Brook, as the flyfishing there is a challenge but worth the effort.

The challenge is twofold. First, the casting is pretty exacting. Often, the stream is quite calm, so a cast that slaps the fly onto the water will spook fish in every direction, putting them all down and making them refuse a fly for many minutes. You learn to cast so that the line straightens out over the water and lands softly, with the fly, leader and line all settling at once. Then, you have to impart some motion to the fly, as the stream is very slow-moving normally, but not so much motion that you sink a dry fly, or make a streamer or wet fly move too quickly.

Because the water is deep, the fish will be coming from a bit of a distance underneath the fly, and so enticing them to hit requires some deftness of flyfishing techniques.

Second is the stream width. There is a small, spring-fed rivulet that enters the main brook at the midsection of the main pool. Often the beavers have this dammed, but always there is a small trickle of very cold water that enters the brook here. The main brook's seventy-foot width, however, creates a cast that most cannot achieve routinely, particularly because of that waist-high grass and the alders that are a bit further back from the stream's edge. A sloppy cast will almost certainly get caught in either the grass or the bushes on the backcast, and a forward cast of seventy feet is something that even the most experienced fly-fisher can do routinely only in ideal circumstances—which almost never occur.

My brother once suggested we bring a ladder in with us, which would probably be worth the effort sometime!

What this all means is that frequently one is making a fifty- or sixty-foot cast and then trying to mend line so that the fly is carried to rises that occur downstream—usually clear across the river, in the pool where the spring enters. When such a cast is made, it almost always pays off.

One early-fall day, I made such an ideal cast and was rewarded with a large trout smashing into the fly. At first, the trout surprised me, coming out of nowhere, and it hit so hard the trout hooked itself, really, as he dove on top of the fly coming clear over it!

The trout then zipped out into the open water to my right, thankfully, as I don't know if I could have held it had it gone up into the beaver choppings and below the dam. The fish went deep down to the bottom of the pool and I could feel it moving rapidly back and forth.

Worried that there might be an obstacle on the bottom, I used my rod tip quite forcefully and managed to get the fish to come back up, but it took line out several times in the fight, as it instinctively tried to get back to the safety of deeper water.

Eventually, I got the trout to swim back toward me, which meant he was fighting both the current and my line. As he tired, he began to swim closer to the surface.

I could see it was a very large brook trout and, carefully, I came from behind it, close to the bank of the stream, with my short-handled net.

This motion almost led to a fishing trip hallmark: I nearly lost my balance when the trout swam slightly away from the bank as I reached out. I managed to avoid a nose-dive and swept the fish into the net.

The trout was a male, in beautiful, bright, breeding colours, with a slightly hooked jaw. He probably measured seventeen inches long. He was as big a native brookie as I'd caught in Yarmouth County.

Harking back to memories of my youth, I held it gently, gazed at the gorgeous markings, and then released it back into the brook. I was gratified that it swam away rapidly, not showing any ill effects from the battle.

I stood there for a few moments contemplating the beauty of a fall day, the water, and the fish, and realized this was indeed a special place.

~

In the early 1980s, this particular watershed faced a challenge. A mining company, Rio Algom, had discovered deposits of tin in the area and in 1984 began a tin-mining operation. There were issues right from the start.

The river was first threatened just from access. The dirt road became a paved highway. The increase in traffic also meant that many more anglers could easily reach Big Meadow Brook.

The stream was impacted negatively by several issues with the mine during the eight years it operated, the most serious being a leak from the tailings pond that caused the entire Tusket from Big Meadow Brook downstream to become very turbid and murky for a number of days.

The flyfishing suffered as the trout began to be affected by overfishing and the environmental issues. At the same time, invasive fish like chain pickerel and smallmouth bass were becoming an issue for the trout in southwestern Nova Scotia.

The tin mine closed in 1992, and to its credit Rio Algom and subsequent owners of the mine did a good job of managing the tailings, preventing further large-scale damage from the mine itself. In fact, the process the mine companies used to treat the tailings piles and the ponds around the mounds became a net positive.

~

In the early 2000s, my brother and I made a flyfishing trip that would make Big Meadow Brook even more special in our memories. We drove to the main river and launched our kayaks at the bottom of the still water.

Paddling to the main pool, we saw many small trout rising and had a ball catching and releasing them. We paddled up through the narrows, where the brook is wedged between two huge boulders, and Bob cast his Professor wet fly beautifully and caught three more small trout in the one spot.

We continued paddling up to the junction of the main brook and another small tributary, a spring-fed stream similar to the one on the main pool. We fly-fished from our kayaks, casting into the opening of the small stream, and handily caught a large number of small trout.

Casting a fly from a kayak is tricky because you can't use your legs at all, but we managed to get close without the small boats causing enough fuss to put the fish down. It is a lot of fun to be sitting below the water level in a small craft that is propelled by a double-bladed paddle.

With memories of our "blue boat" days dancing in our heads, we then paddled far upstream, to where Duck Pond Brook empties into Big Meadow Brook. Again, we saw numerous rises of small fish, and managed to catch and release many—none bigger than eight inches.

On the way back downstream, Bob mentioned that we had seen a lot of small brook trout, but hadn't seen any really big ones. This got me thinking, and over the next year or so, our chapter of Trout Unlimited Canada (TUC) took an interest in ways to improve the flyfishing at Big Meadow Brook.

My friend and chapter vice-president at the time, Steve Adams, and I spoke to the Trout Unlimited biologist for Ontario, who visited us. And it was then that we realized what was happening.

The mining operation involved a tailings mound, or mounds, that extended for a distance long enough to be visible from the air. These huge mounds of disturbed earth were being managed by the companies, and they were surrounded by a system of moats and ponds that collected the rainwater that ran off the piles of earth. The companies then conducted chemical analysis and treated the water to make it more natural. One of the things they did was to add lime to the water to neutralize the pH level.

Since the water in most of Yarmouth County drains from peat bogs and swamps, the natural pH of that water is low to begin with. During the 1970s, acid rain took a heavy toll on freshwater sport fish like salmon and trout.

Here, then, was a company that had signed a contract that had it treating the water before releasing it through Duck Pond Brook and into the main Big Meadow Brook. The water, because it was treated for pH, was the most neutral water in Yarmouth County—and was a breeding ground for brook trout! The overfishing had simply exposed the other side of the problem: so many people were fishing here that the trout never grew to be large, and so breeding fish were more rare, and those that did breed did so earlier, and at a smaller size than before.

Our chapter of TUC contacted the Department of Inland Fisheries, and with their help we began a project in which we surveyed people using a volunteer creel survey on the size and number of fish they were catching. When this confirmed our hypothesis, the government and our chapter, backed by TUC nationally, made Big Meadow Brook a Special Trout Management Area—one of the first of its kind in western Nova Scotia.

The regulations were changed so that Big Meadow Brook became catch and release only, and the use of natural bait is prohibited; you can only use lures and flyfishing to catch the trout. The idea, of course, is that by preserving the brook trout that are in the watershed, they eventually will grow larger and there can be a blue-ribbon trout fishery in an area that now is known more for the smallmouth bass fishing.

Today, when one goes fishing at Big Meadow Brook, the fish are larger and just as numerous as they were before. I have yet to catch another seventeen-inch fall brook trout, but that is the hope for the future. That, alongside the hope that the pickerel don't make it that far upriver, but it may be only a matter of time and, in the end, we may have simply bought the system some time without the changes that the invasive species will bring.

Still, the effort is worth it because this is really what conservation is about, trying to save what we have so that future generations, like my grandson Theo, can fish at places like Big Meadow Brook and have those special experiences.

~

A bit of bad news as an epilogue to this chapter is necessary. In the two years since I began writing this book, things have not gone well for Big Meadow, and this reflects the issue with invasive species in the western end of Nova Scotia.

Almost two years ago, just after having completed the draft for this work, I fished one early May day at Big Meadow with a friend who was new to fly fishing in this area.

We walked in along the path to stand at the middle of the main pool, a place I have guided people to for decades. The early spring air was fresh with the smell of the shad bushes (serviceberries), and we had seen hatches of mayflies earlier in the area.

We fished for about a half hour, but saw nothing rising at all, on what should have been a perfect day for surface action. Many times, when this happens it means that the trout have become full on a hatch from earlier in the day, or they may be feeding on nymphs that are not near the surface.

Leaving my friend at the main pool, I began walking—well, wading really, as the marsh grass was covered by some water from a rain earlier that week—downstream toward where the car was parked.

As I rounded the large bend in the river that leads down to the lower pool, I saw a rise—a very large circle of rings where a fish had just been feeding on something. I made a couple of false casts; casting, but not actually letting the fly hit the water, to extend the length of line out that I would need to place a fly near the rise.

My first true cast was still a bit short, so I lifted the fly line off the water quickly, and with as little disturbance as possible. My second cast was perfect, landing just upstream from the now larger circles, but the current and my mending meant the fly drifted just upstream of where the fish had been near the surface.

As I began to pull the fly line in to make the Muddler Minnow I was using move, a fish erupted, breaking the surface, coming clear up and smashing back down, taking the fly in its mouth and then turning downstream.

I played the fish carefully but quickly as, with the rules in place, catch and release is the only allowed method of fishing and I did not want to tire the fish out and lower the odds of its survival afterwards. I soon had a beautiful 17 inch trout in hand – a dark coloured brook trout that would probably be four or five years old.

Thrilled, as this was the actual in-the-hand evidence of the wisdom of our efforts as conservationists, I was even more gratified when I caught another trout, almost the twin of the first, in the pool downstream as my friend and I walked out of Big Meadow.

My brother Bob came up that summer, and of course he'd heard about the large trout in May, so we wanted to see if the same thing would hold for August. On a soft mid-August morning, we made the drive to Big Meadow in my hybrid Rav 4 with my big canoe on top.

Our idea was to paddle up-river to get a good feel for what state the system was in, and Bob, being the keen ornithologist, also wanted to see what birds might be around.

We paddled through the lower pool, where just three months ago I'd taken the large trout, through the main pool and then began our paddle well upstream. We flushed a number of ducks and other waterfowl, saw kingfishers and warblers and even spotted a couple of beavers; but oddly, on such a perfect day, saw not a single fish rising as we paddled up to the very headwaters of the system.

Turning back downstream we made it to well below the Duck Pond brook before I finally raised a fish by casting my fly into the mouth of a small rivulet. I missed the fish, and Bob then cast immediately behind my rise. He had a fish chase his fly, take it and turn, and we both knew instantly what it was—a chain pickerel.

We were both heart-broken to see this fish in a system we love, as with the deep, slow characteristics of Big Meadow, it's a prime place for pickerel to succeed simply by eating any smaller fish, mainly the brook trout we've all worked so hard to protect and nurture.

I have to admit that, last summer, for the first time in over 60 years, I did not go to Big Meadow.

As I wrote in my diary: *Phooey*.

8: Marrying into flyfishing

Figure 11: Cape Smokey

I met Norma at Acadia University, and we dated. Being two years older than me, she graduated and went off to work in Middle Musquodoboit as a teacher, while I finished my studies in Wolfville. Somehow, we stayed together through those two years, and then it was time that I should meet her parents.

We drove to Cape Breton, where Norma had been born and raised. I was nervous during the drive, as any prospective suitor would be. Norma's family was only three generations Canadian. Her grandmother was fluently bilingual and spoke either English or Gaelic, the family having come to Canada in the 1800s from the Isle of Skye in Scotland.

Her grandmother took one look at me in my jeans and—in my defence—a good shirt, and declared in Gaelic that I was a "scruff," as was later translated to me.

Norma's parents, I am happy to say, had other opinions. Norma's mother was a warm and welcoming person, who I later learned had checked me out a bit through mutual friends of theirs and my parents. Em and Norman had learned my family were "nice people" and that I was probably okay.

The perils of dating an only child became obvious to me quite quickly. Norm, as he preferred to be called, discovered that I enjoyed the outdoors (Norma had primed her parents, I suspect). When he learned I enjoyed flyfishing, well, that was good, something to investigate.

And investigate we did.

From that weekend on, for almost thirty years until Norm passed away just shy of his ninetieth birthday, he and I would explore the woods and waters of Cape Breton Island and beyond. This northernmost region of Nova Scotia became like a second home for me, and I suspect I know the flyfishing there as well as, or better than, most native-born Capers, because my learning occurred at the feet of someone who knew the Island so well.

Naturally, the fact Norm had lived and fly-fished in Cape Breton all his life did lead to some indelibly memorable incidents.

We would frequently go to a spot he'd say he'd been to that had good fishing "once before." I learned after a few of these "hot tips" to ask, "Was that before the war or after the war?" Sometimes, in the 1980s or 1990s, we'd show up at a place and he couldn't understand how it had become so grown over since he last had been there, but that may have been before the war, in the late 1930s!

Norm did know the Island well, though, and he led me to some wonderful flyfishing spots, where we enjoyed amazingly good fishing and warm fellowship. Norm had a gang of men friends who fished, and most were fly fishermen. Often when Norma and I arrived for a visit, Norm would have a recommendation of where to go based on some knowledge passed on by one of these friends.

I should mention that Norm was an optometrist by training, and a visit to the eye doctor for many of his friends was a great chance to talk flyfishing.

The first trip we took together was in April, when Norma and I went to visit her parents for Easter. This timing meant that, in Cape Breton, the ice had barely left the lakes, although it also meant the brooks and rivers would be torrents.

Norm had heard from a friend that the fishing was good in Lake Ainslie, one of Nova Scotia's largest lakes, on the western side of Cape Breton. Norm and his family had camped there when Norma was a small child, so he knew the lake well. We would be fishing out of his aluminum boat, which was different for me, as we normally fly-fished by wading or from a canoe or kayak.

At the lake, we launched at the campground and motored out to where Norm thought we might find some fish. We were both enveloped in warm clothes, Norm in his trademark snowmobile suit, and me in my ski outfit, a parka and an old pair of ski pants.

To his credit, Norm was always quite safety-conscious about some aspects of boating, and so we had on-board PFDs, and we both wore them.

Norm was not so conscious about another safety aspect: he did like to have a "wee drop" while on these outdoor adventures. On this trip, he'd brought along some bottles of beer, although I now know he probably also had his flask on his person somewhere; in the years to come, I realized he seldom left home without it! Not that he'd be drinking all the time, no, just that he was of such Scottish descent that the Boy Scouts would be proud: he was always prepared!

As we absentmindedly fished the lake, Norm asked if I'd like a beer; we hadn't seen much action that day. I said sure, and we sipped quietly for a bit.

When Norm finished his beer, he did something that horrified me: he leaned over the side of the boat, filled the empty beer bottle with lake water, and let it sink into the depths.

I gasped and said, "Oh, I wish you wouldn't do that!"

Now, in my defence, I'd been brought up in Groton, Massachusetts, a town that had the Nashua River running right through it. In high school in 1970, I'd been the president of an environment club that had participated in the very first Earth Day.

I had been raised by my mother's step-mom to question authority if I saw pollution or other things that were damaging to the Earth—even if it meant confronting my grandfather, as the school's environment club did in the ensuing river clean-up. When I was at Lawrence Academy, the Nashua would turn the colour of whatever paper my grandfather's company, Groton Leatherboard, was using that day to produce their products.

At one time, the Nashua was rated as one of the ten most polluted streams in the United States; today, one can swim and fish in it. Conservation has always been in my nature.

Norm looked at me quizzically but didn't say anything.

I knew I'd stepped on his toes, so I quickly changed the subject. "Look, bald eagles over there," I said.

"There are lots of eagles on Lake Ainslie," Norm began. "I remember one time when Wally and I were fishing here—"

I was safe. Norm was off with one of his stories.

My conservation ways did rub off on Norm eventually, though. One memorable afternoon we were fishing on Middle River, a stream that is among my favourites to fly-fish, and the run of sea trout was in. Norm wanted to fish the main pool in this midsection of the river and said I should go upstream to fish the upper pools and work my way down to him; he'd simply wait for me at the large lower pool.

I walked upstream and began fishing the upper couple of pools. Since the run was in, I had very good flyfishing in each spot. As a result, it took me two hours or more to fish down to where Norm was patiently standing on the bank of the river at the top of the main pool.

As I worked my way down to him, I noticed that, while we were each hooking, playing, and releasing many trout, Norm would occasionally wade out of the water, walk to the top of the pool, look at something on the riverbank, and then return to where he had been fishing.

It seemed a bit odd, but maybe he was changing flies or fixing his leader, I thought. I knew there had to be an explanation.

The answer to the riddle became evident as I rounded the last bend in the river, just above where the main Middle River flow curved away from a large bank, with trees overhanging it and a deep pool to cast into. As I was fishing this run just above the main pool, I could more clearly see Norm flyfishing.

He was casting his Grasshopper wet fly across the stream and letting the current take the fly quickly through the top of the pool but then slow as the fly got downstream from where he was standing. The fly was now fully across the river and paralleling a rock-strewn bank with dozens of places a trout could hide. As well, the pool here was at its deepest, so some larger fish would be waiting below.

Norm hooked a good sea trout, silver and bright, just as I approached the top run of the main pool. The trout hit hard and was hooked well, and it swam deeply at first with the current, putting on quite the show by stripping line as it went, and then turning into the flow and slowly working its way upstream as Norm led the fish back toward him. The shingle on the side of the river where Norm was standing was clear rocks, so there was no worry about snagging anything, other than if he allowed the fish to go deeper into the main pool and swim around the odd stump that laid below.

Norm worked the trout up toward where he stood, and then, with a deft tug, slid the fish up onto the rocky bank. It was then that I could discern the answer to the goings-on I had witnessed from above.

Norm unhooked the fish and put his fly rod down. He walked up toward me, and stopped ten or so yards away. I could see an odd-shaped set of rocks where Norm was now leaning over, just on the river's edge.

Norm had built what in essence was a holding pen! He looked up and for the first time spotted me standing upstream. "I have four nice fish in my creel," he said, "and I want to only keep the biggest for my fifth."

Norm was cycling his catch! He would take the just-caught trout up to his holding pool, where the rocks created a small dam and made a pool deep enough to let a trout swim, but not escape, and then he would estimate whether the current resident of the holding pool was bigger or smaller than the fish in hand. If the fish in the pool was smaller, he replaced it with the larger fish, if larger, the fish in hand went gently back into the river.

I laughed to myself, as in previous years Norm would have thought nothing of bending the rules and catching five fish—the limit at the time —having a shore lunch of those trout, and then fishing for five more to take home. Not technically legal, but in the days when the sea trout ran so thickly that catching a hundred trout in a morning was not uncommon, I suppose it can be excused.

In any case, this holding pool idea was at least advancing his actions toward legality.

This time I only said, "Nice fish, there," and left him to his fun.

Norm and I had many adventures in the ensuing years. On one occasion, we fished North River, also in Cape Breton. At Norm's insistence we had walked the four miles up to the very headwaters that we were allowed to fish on that stream. The idea, I guess, was that since the sea trout had come in a couple of weeks before, maybe they'd all run up to the top of the river.

It was a sound plan, and the walk along this gorgeous river was most enjoyable. We saw glimpses of the river below as we walked the trail on the north side of the river, up past an old abandoned farm, and then up to the very top pools of the river.

Norm's idea was that we'd fish down the stream, so we didn't fish going up; we simply walked.

We got set to fish once we hit the farthest upstream we could go, which was a spot just below a pretty good-sized waterfall.

Unfortunately, neither of us had checked the weather forecast carefully, and, as we finally began to set up to begin our fishing, we heard a rumble of thunder in the distance. Soon, the clouds thickened and darkened, and it began to rain.

Now, fishing in the rain was nothing new to either of us; in fact, sometimes the flyfishing in a rainstorm can be quite good, as the fish can't see as easily with the rain dimpling the water's surface.

Suddenly, though, the thunder grew much closer, and we saw flashes of lightning. Knowing that we were quite high up North Mountain, and on a ridge, no less, we took the obvious precautions. Heading slightly downstream, we got lower to the water in a small ravine, and huddled down under a small stand of low spruce.

Soon, the lightning was all around us, working its way down the river! We both held our breath as the storm raged all around us, but as quickly as it began, the squall passed us and rumbled on downriver.

We emerged from beneath the bushes, and went to pick up the fly rods we'd left nearer to the stream.

"That was quite close," said Norm, in the understatement of all time. "I wonder if that'll put the fish down?"

~

Norm's adventurous spirit often meant we would travel all over the Island looking for trout spots he'd heard about. The routine became that Norma and I would arrive at her parents' place for a weekend or during a school break, and Norm would spend the first evening telling me all about the spots he'd received tips on. We'd be up early the next morning, and off we'd go, looking for whatever fish Norm's clients or friends had told him about.

Sometimes this method introduced me to new things, like the time we unintentionally went squid fishing. Norm had heard the mackerel were running in the bay in front of the old farm in St. Anns that the family owned, so that morning we set out and launched the small homemade boat in the little pond in front of the old farmhouse.

The boat is a story all by itself. It was a gorgeous little Mahone Bay–style sixteen-footer, very deep and very heavy. Norm had built the craft the year Em was pregnant with Norma, during the first full year of their marriage. He had built it in their kitchen, which meant that, for the duration of Em's pregnancy, the kitchen was home to two growing figures.

Norma was born in January. The boat, which had to go out through the kitchen bay window (the window and casing being removed), Norm having misjudged the clearance required for the boat to fit through the doorway, was shoved outside in March.

The bay window was replaced, and Norm's boat proved to be watertight and suitable for fishing.

This particular day, having launched the boat, we motored out into St. Ann's Bay, in a bit of a chop. The small craft bounced a little, but we did see mackerel and managed to catch a few on our spinning rods.

Norm decided he'd try his handline for a bit. The rig consisted of very heavy line—it may have been two-hundred–pound test nylon, like you'd use for tuna.

In fact, that may have been where he'd gotten it, as Bluefin tuna fishermen came to St. Anns for sport and often lost gear to the giant fish, which would wash up on the beach in front of the farm. Norm, being the type to never let anything go to waste, devised a use for the heavy line. On the inboard end, Norm had wrapped the line around a very heavy two-handed spool, shaped like the letter *H*, which he could let spin on two small handles on the sides. The fishing end had the heavy line tied to a long leader of maybe fifty-pound test nylon, onto which were tied half a dozen quite large flies—orange and red saltwater hooks dressed like Mickey Finn wet flies. The flies were connected to another short length of leader and below that was a two-pound lead weight.

The flyfishing method would be to drop the flies and the weight overboard and let the spool spin out until the weight hit bottom, and then he'd simply retrieve the whole affair by winding the line back onto the spool by hand, sometimes stopping a bit and jigging the line up and down to entice more mackerel to hit.

It was an effective, if not very nuanced, system, and often Norm would haul in three or more mackerel at once. We soon had a five-gallon bucket full of the dark silvery fish.

I was having fun with my small spinning outfit and lighter gear, as the mackerel were a pretty good size and fun to catch as they fought well.

After an hour or so, Norm was not catching as many mackerel at once as he would have liked, so we moved the boat, and he dropped the flies down in a new spot. As he retrieved the line he said, "Oh, must have a couple on here."

When he started bringing the flies over the side of the boat, we were both quickly covered with gooey black ink which was squirting everywhere! Norm had every hook filled with squid, and as they were lifted over the side of the boat, each shot a stream of ink as it flipped over the rail and onto the floorboards.

"You can't eat them, but they make good bait," said Norm.

He'd never heard of calamari, and since I thought only of eels, I didn't ever tell him.

Our explorations did, however, lead us to find some wonderful trout flyfishing, and seemed often to entail driving around Cape Breton Island just for the sake of driving around the Island, something Norm loved to do.

One of his favourite spots, that he learned of from a good friend and client, was where the South West Margaree exits Lake Ainslie under a little iron bridge as it runs through a narrowing that causes a pool at the lake's exit, and then a series of runs before the river flows more gently down below through numerous meadows and glades. There had been an old sawmill there, so the pool on top was named the Sawdust Pile.

The deep pool had a very soft bottom, as the rock was covered by a thick layer of old wood shavings and sawdust; but where the stream began to pick up speed and run into the rapids, the bottom was firm and easily waded. We'd start at the Sawdust Pile, and often we'd spot trout hitting dry flies, sucking in the insects as the current softly carried them out of the lake and downstream.

Norm frequently spent the entire time fishing just that pool with dry flies, while I would take my Muddler Minnow and fish the running water. Norm, wearing his chest waders, loved being up to his waist in water, thus at eye level with the fish as they dimpled the water. He would cast gently to them.

This often meant a fishing trip would occur spontaneously, as sometimes he'd misjudge the depth just a hair, and the stream would begin flowing into his waders, but he never really seemed to mind, because he'd be intently casting to a rise.

Figure 12: Some of Norm's flies

In his later years, Norm learned to fly-fish out of a kayak, and I think he enjoyed it very much in part because of the same connection to the fish—being low and being able to get close to them—instead of using the motorboat he'd always used, which was effective transportation, but the motor would put the fish down.

I'd be having fun casting downstream through the small pools and backwaters, picking the spots I thought a trout should be lying. Often, they would co-operate and take my fly as it swung by a large rock or as the fly would be swept over a ridge of rocks and into a small pool.

These were lovely, large trout, averaging maybe twelve or thirteen inches. They'd be fat, and silver from the salt water they had gone out to, and they'd be good fighters.

But, even if the sea-run wasn't in, there would be many native brook trout, smaller but willing to hit my fly, and in running water sometimes just as much fun on light fly gear as their bigger brethren.

Norm seemed to enjoy flyfishing at the other end of the province as well. One spring, for the opening of the season, Dad and I were going to go to Deerfield to open up the cottage. Since it was Easter weekend, Norm and Em had come to visit Norma and me at our home in Lockeport.

Of course, Dad and I invited Norm along for the fun. Norm knew Dad was a fly fisherman, but Norm also had a bit of my grandfather's "use whatever works" spirit, and he'd brought along his spinning gear just in case.

The weekend dawned bright and with a gentle west wind, but it was cold, with the temperature hovering a few degrees below freezing; in fact the lakes were still frozen up.

We drove from the cottage toward Kempt. The first stream we came to that had good open water was the Tusket, as it flowed from a series of lakes through a narrow, shallow gorge and under the old bridge in Carleton. The spot was perfect for several anglers at once as the river went under the bridge and then fanned out into several small, shallow branches, making little rapids and runs in several different directions.

I began by using my trusty Muddler Minnow on the far right side of the rapids, Dad went to the little island in the centre with his Mickey Finn, and Norm waded out to the left side, which is the main channel, and fished there with his Grasshopper.

All three of us became a bit frustrated because it was so cold that, on the retrieve back, the fly line deposited water that froze almost instantly onto the guides of the rod, making retrieving line and working the fly a misery. None of us caught anything, mainly because it was so difficult to work the relatively thick fly lines back onto the reel or even use our hands to get enough in to make an effective cast.

After a half hour, Dad stopped fishing and went to sit in the truck, and I joined him a few minutes later. We were both not only frustrated; we were cold.

When Norm noticed we weren't in the stream with him, he came to the window of the truck to ask if we were staying. Dad said he wasn't sure it was worth trying here any longer, or other places either, as it was so cold.

Norm said, "Well, if we're staying here a few minutes, I'll try my spinning rod."

Dad and I sat in the truck in our jeans and heavy sweaters and nylon jackets and watched as Norm, ensconced in a snowmobile suit complete with thickly-insulated winter boots, happily waded back to the shallow run on the left side. He tossed a lure, a small red-and-white spoon, into the current.

We noticed that with the spinning rod he didn't have the line freezing issues, or at least not to the extent that it interfered much with the fishing.

On the third or fourth cast Norm hooked a trout, a dandy fish that hit the spoon hard, then turned and went with the current down into the deeper pool.

Norm excitedly played the fish for several minutes, getting it to stay in front of him, and not allowing it to swim over to the island Dad had been fishing, where there was a lot of brush and deadwood in the stream to snag a line on. He eventually got the trout up onto the rocky shingle above the island and beached it quickly (none of us had a net).

Norm then did something that I think was quite new to him. He picked the fish up gently, and looked at it for a second or two, and then gently released it back into the river.

He clambered up the bank and came to the truck window on my side. "First fish of the season always goes back, right?" he asked with a broad smile. "That's the family rule, isn't it?"

You see, over time, my conservation ethic indeed rubbed off on him, and I also became the son he'd never had.

9: Salmon flyfishing

Figure 13: Margaree River

The Atlantic salmon possesses a mystique to many, and indeed it is a fish worthy of such regard. Salmon in Nova Scotia are considered the king of game fish, in freshwater anyway, and they can be caught legally only on a fly.

To call oneself a salmon angler means one has to both be a fly-fisher and be able to work larger flies for bigger and much more powerful fish.

My very first witness to a salmon in hand was not a legal take.

I was perhaps seven years old at the time and was still using a bait outfit, while Dad fished with his fly rod. We headed to a spot above a still water lake on Salmon River, just above the Highway 3 bridge, past the salmon hole my grandfather used to call the Red Barn Pool and down a short dirt lane to where the main river went under a farmer's small wooden bridge.

The bridge was very simple, a few wide, rough-cut timbers across a frame, as it merely served to get that farmer's tractor to the fields and woods on the opposite side of the stream, but that made the bridge perfect as a rough fishing platform.

As we approached the bridge, we could see another fisherman there, sitting in the middle with some fish laid out across the span next to him while he fished with a worm and bobber. He had maybe ten fish lying there (the limit in those days was fifteen), and he chatted as we approached.

"Good fishing here today," he said.

"How long have you been fishing?" asked Dad.

"Oh, about a half hour," the man said, "but these guys bite pretty quickly as a small school goes through."

"That's a nice mess of fish you've got there," Dad stated.

"Yes, salmon trout are my favourite," the man replied.

There was a run of immature salmon, salmon parr they are called, fish that are descending the river for the first time and heading out to sea. The man had caught his ten fish, all about the same seven- to nine-inch size and had created—in his mind and hopefully for the authorities if questioned—a new species of trout to explain keeping what were clearly illegal salmon.

Dad and I left promptly, I assume so as not to be implicated in any wrongdoing should an RCMP officer or DNR warden pass by.

When I was about ten, Dad was fishing the outflow of our brook at the cottage, the pool just above the old mill dam. I was with a friend, riding our bikes up the dirt road past my uncle's cottage, when we heard my Dad shout, "Boys! Can you go get Grampy's net from the pump house?"

From where we were standing on the bank of the road, which was elevated well above the river, we could see Dad had hooked a large salmon in the small pool and was engaged in an epic battle to try to keep the fish from running under the alders or down over the dam spillway, either of which would have assured losing the fish.

I tore up the lane on my bike to our cottage, dashed into the pump house to grab the long-handled dip net, and pedalled furiously back to Dad.

I arrived just in time to see the fish take a quick run downstream toward the spillway, while Dad worked the fish with his rod to make it turn so it didn't go downstream further, but it got too near the far shore. Just as I was descending the bank toward the pool, net clutched in hand, the fish took a mighty leap upstream and actually cleared a branch of an overhanging maple, looping the line over the limb. Upon coming back down into the water, it swam directly downstream, causing the line to break.

Dad stared blankly at the parted line, and then turned to me and said, "Well, that was fun!"

I nodded in agreement, but I would very much have liked to help land a salmon.

~

While in university I didn't do any salmon fishing, but we did come upon one accidentally once.

Wayne, Chris, and I were fishing a small stream that was a headwater for the LaHave River, which was a very good salmon stream in its day. We had gone flyfishing this day in early May, scouting for worthwhile trout spots when the big hatches would come later that month.

Wayne had ventured out in his chest waders almost crotch-deep when a fish inhaled his fly. He raised his rod tip and, although he had hooked what was obviously a big fish, it didn't fight much.

We were all perplexed as to what manner of piscatorial beast this might turn out to be, but it didn't take long to find out. After a few minutes of rather lethargic play, Wayne brought a very dark Atlantic salmon to hand. It was close to thirty inches long, but instead of weighing the twelve pounds or so it would normally have weighed, this fish couldn't have gone to more than six or seven pounds.

The salmon was a kelt, or slink, salmon, a breeding adult that had spawned and overwintered in the fresh water and was now heading downriver to get back to the sea.

Wayne handled the fish carefully, not lifting it out of the water, and we all admired it for a moment. He then released the fish, holding it lightly just in front of the tail and letting it recover in the gently flowing water.

As Wayne released the fish, I commented that the next time we would see that fish, it would be a huge multi-year breeder. As renowned fly fisherman Lee Wulff famously said, "A salmon is too valuable to be caught but once!"

Figure 14: An Orange Parson

Atlantic salmon were so common In Nova Scotia in the 1920s and 1930s that the woodsmen had it written into their employment contracts that salmon could be served to them at the logging camps no more than three times a week! By the 1980s, when Norma and I moved to Lockeport after university, things had begun to change in southwestern Nova Scotia, what used to be the heart of the best salmon fishing area of the province.

With acid rain, the Atlantic salmon, even more sensitive to acid waters than the brook trout, began to decline in numbers. The damming of river sheds to provide hydropower also negatively impacted these fish, which need free access to the shallow gravel breeding grounds far upstream.

When you add in clear-cut logging operations, coal-burning power plants, and other polluting activity, the salmon in Nova Scotia had the deck stacked against their long-term survival. This also explains why, to this day, the clearer, limestone and gypsum streams of Cape Breton hold more salmon than the southern half of the province, where the naturally acidic peat bog–draining rivers are marginal habitat to begin with.

Still, there was some Atlantic salmon fishing to be had in the southwest, and since I lived there, I wanted to take advantage of it and learn about it.

My first experience with Atlantic salmon outside of Yarmouth County, and the first salmon I caught myself, confirmed for me that salmon fishing was something worth working at, and it also greatly enhanced my desire to learn as much as I could about flyfishing.

Gren Jones, a friend from the Annapolis Valley, lived across the river from my parents' farm near Canning. He was raised in Queens County, just across the county line from where Norma and I found ourselves. Lockeport is in the extreme east end of Shelburne County, and Gren's family's home was in Hunts Point, in the extreme western end of Queens County.

Gren's dad, who knew a lot of local guides, had arranged for Gren to go fishing on the Medway River in early June. Gren called me and asked if I'd like to be the second sport in the boat. Of course, I agreed instantly.

The night before our trip, Norma and I camped in a small campground near Greenfield so that I would be on time and fresh for the fishing. Gren met me at the guide's home, a small bungalow along the river.

The guide, Clyde Croft, was a wonderful man and a great flyfishing guide. Gren's father knew Clyde well, and it was Gren's dad who suggested that we should employ Clyde's services for the day.

We had arrived early in the morning, and were promptly escorted to Clyde's fishing boat, a classic eighteen-foot punt that he would pole across the river using a long pole instead of a paddle as you would use in a canoe. Clyde placed me in the bow and Gren amidships, and Clyde took the stern, holding a twelve-foot long stout pole.

Clyde swung the boat upstream and allowed it to drift across the river. He anchored it so that the stern swung pointing upstream, which meant I had the prime spot in the bow, which now faced the pool below which he wished us to fish.

The pool was in a section of the Medway that was not exactly fast water, but it did have a fairly good run to it. There were large boulders on both the right-hand side looking downstream, near the far bank, and in the middle of the river, which meant the water flowed into a *V* shape between several big rocks before it flattened out more to become the main pool.

"We'll work the top of the pool, and fish down below later," said Clyde. "The fish will be just below the boulders where that smooth water is." The man certainly knew the pool well.

I simply had to cast a relatively short line, maybe thirty feet, and then let the stream carry the fly down into the spot Clyde was describing. Clyde had looked over our flies earlier, and had given each of us a "Croft Special"—a number 4 salmon fly of his own invention, tied with a red body and gold ribbing, and with a wing of brown deer hair. A rather plainly dressed fly, as far as salmon flies go, but again, the man knew the pool. (In later years, I would learn that this was a simple tie of the traditional Copper Killer salmon fly.)

Gren and I fished for perhaps twenty minutes. I allowed my fly to swing straight downstream from the boat, while Gren cast cleanly across the stream and then picked up his fly as it swung level with the large boulder below us. I worked my fly so that it would swim from just below the boulder, across the flowing water and then through to the pool below, where it slowed and sank more deeply.

As I cast out toward the large boulder, I saw a rise just in the middle of the slack water at the top of the pool below me.

"Did you see that?" Clyde asked.

"Yes, I did," I replied, now engrossed in trying to get my line back to hand to where I could make a mended cast.

Figure 15: A Croft Special

"Cast across, though, and let it sink a bit," Clyde instructed.

It took a lot of willpower not to just cast right at the rise, but if I had done so, the fly would have been swimming on the surface of the water, and it would have been moving very quickly through the pool. As usual, Clyde was correct.

As my cast went out, I could see another rise below the one we saw earlier.

"Wow," I said.

"Cool," muttered Gren.

As my line came to a halt straight below me, I felt a sudden tug. I raised my tip, and the rod bent almost in half. A very bright salmon grilse, just in out of the sea, had hit the fly and had turned downstream, taking the line right out of my hand and now was stripping line furiously off the reel.

Fortunately, the fish did not go downstream from the main pool below, but instead, upon reaching the lower edge of the pool, it jumped twice in quick succession and then shot back upstream. Winding my reel as quickly as I could, I managed to keep up with the fish, and soon it was nearing the boat.

The pool where we were anchored was quite deep, so the first time the fish came near us, it went under the punt in maybe eight feet of water. The salmon swam briefly upstream of the boat before being turned by my rod pressure and, more likely, by the stream's flow.

Now back in the main pool, the fish was simply swimming back and forth, so both my line and the current were working to tire it out.

"See if you can bring him up here again," said Clyde, as he traded spots with Gren so that he was now right behind my left shoulder.

I did as instructed and the fish swam upstream, this time much nearer to the surface.

In a move that I'd seen my grandfather do a hundred times, Clyde came from behind the fish with his long-handled dip net, brought the bag of the net upward, and swung the net inboard. My first Atlantic salmon lay gasping in the bottom of the boat with the fly still embedded firmly in the corner of its mouth.

Reaching down to release the fly, Clyde said, "That's a lovely grilse. You'll want to keep that one, I expect."

I said I would indeed, as I admired the silvery scales glistening in the sunlight. The fish weighed about five pounds, so this was a mature first-year sea fish, a salmon that had been out to sea for one year and was probably returning to breed for the first time.

"Why don't you and Gren trade spots," Clyde suggested.

I agreed, thinking it would be great to see Gren catch a salmon as well.

I was almost absent-mindedly casting across toward the large boulder and letting my fly swim across the quick current, while Gren more intently cast to the same pool I had just been fishing. We could still see fish rising occasionally in both the main pool and the backwater behind the boulder.

Deciding that I'd challenge myself with a longer cast, I let out a bit more line as my fly went downstream. I brought the line in and prepared to cast so that my fly would land behind the boulder on the far side of the stream from us.

The cast worked better than I thought, and as I sat there watching the fly swirl past the little eddy and come up just along the backwards flow, where it would have eventually been carried by the bending line downstream much further and much more rapidly, the unexpected happened.

The small backwater erupted as a salmon hit my fly, coming up out of the water, and carried it hard down as the fish crashed back into the water just behind the rock, making a huge splash. This meant we all got a good look at the fish—a very large, fully mature, Atlantic salmon!

My line ripped from my hands and the reel unwound much more briskly than with the grilse. The line going through the water actually made a *zipping* sound as the fish made a mad dash downstream, and then, reaching the bottom of the pool, it turned and began running upstream.

The salmon went deeply into the main pool, and then swam rapidly to come even with our boat, maybe six feet below the surface, and it then turned and began to swim straight away from me, back toward the large boulder where it had taken the fly.

"Drop your tip," Clyde yelled from right behind me.

I did, and at just that moment the fish came cleanly out of the water in a graceful arc, about three feet into the air. The line held, because, as Clyde told me later, I bowed to the fish.

The salmon then swam back upstream, turning toward our boat, and it was now visible to each of us.

"That's a big fish," Clyde said, "maybe twenty pounds!"

The fish turned almost as suddenly as it had turned upstream to run quickly back down into the main pool. Unfortunately, it was on a trajectory to wrap the line on the far side of the boulder across the stream.

"Try to keep him from going over there," Clyde advised.

I lifted my rod tip a bit more, but that just caused the fish to dart forward. As it swam past the boulder, the line caught on the side, and the leader broke off!

"Ahhh..." I began to moan.

"Not many get to fight a fish that large," Clyde said. "That there is what we call a 'quick release.' You just let him go out there instead of releasing him in here."

It didn't make me feel much better just then, but it was a fun fight.

I would also mention that, before we left for the day, just before lunch, I caught another grilse, except that would be too mean to Gren, who didn't have a single hit.

I gave Gren the second fish to take home, and his dad informed me later that it was very tasty.

~

With the newly-acquired salmon fishing fever still raging, I went to Cape Breton that summer, and Norm was ecstatic. While he liked to fish for trout, for any fish really, his passion was salmon fishing.

Norm told me about the very good salmon fishing to be had in the Margaree, a river that is without a doubt Nova Scotia's most famous salmon stream. That summer, we fished the Margaree a number of times, but had no luck. We saw some beautiful pools and did see some fish, but other than a rise or two that Norm got at the Hatchery pool, we didn't see much action.

We heard one day of someone who'd fished the North River and caught a salmon, so Norm and I decided on a change of venue.

We parked at the picnic ground at the midpoint of North River's fishable stretch for salmon, just above the ridge that leads down to where the river goes over the "lower" falls. We walked carefully down the path from the parking area to the river, a distance of not more than two hundred yards, but very steep terrain as North River cuts through a gorge the water made in its coursing down from the Highlands plateau above.

At the bottom of the trail, we were standing beside a salmon pool known locally as the Ledge—so named because two very large, flat rocks jut out into the river, causing the flow to bend around the rocks and creating a large deep pool just downstream of the structure. One can stand on the level rocks and be completely dry. In fact, you could stand there in sneakers, and yet you are fishing in twelve or more feet of deep, clear water just in front of you!

Just upstream of the Ledge is a small, steep set of rapids, and above that another pool where the river flowing east hits a solid granite rock face and turns north in a sharp left, ninety-degree turn. This pool, the Upper Ledge Pool, is much shallower, but because one has to scramble upstream a bit and still wade knee-deep or more across a *V* of rocks at the top of the pool, it is obviously less heavily fished than the much more easily accessed Ledge Pool.

Norm decided he would fish from the Ledge, and he let me do the scrambling up to the Upper Ledge Pool this day. Norm, looking down into the clear, still water below the Ledge, could not see any fish, but he began casting anyway and was working the far side of the pool where the current swept his fly away from the boulders across the river and through the deep water below the Ledge itself.

I waded upstream, and as I began to get positioned in the middle of the shallow flow above the upper pool, I saw motion in the water just downstream. I was in luck: there was at least one fish in the Upper Ledge Pool!

I had already tied on a number 4 General Practitioner, a brightly-dressed, orange-coloured classic salmon wet fly. The day was sunny and the water clear, so I was going by my grandfather's standard advice, "Bright day, bright fly; dull day, dull fly."

I cast twice to the right-hand side of the pool but could not get my fly to swim properly with the current to float near to the fish I'd seen—the current was too fast. Taking a chance on spooking the fish, I cast directly above the spot I thought it was lying in, which allowed the leader to straighten, and the fly sank a bit and went straight out and through the pool.

As the fly, now almost directly below me, was beginning to rise in the water column, the fish rose and struck at it. I quickly twitched the tip of my fly rod, and the light-weight rod bent under the weight of the fish and the current.

The salmon darted toward me at first, and then, sensing that continuing in that direction would mean swimming in quite shallow water, it turned and went to the far end of the Upper Ledge Pool, against the granite face of the cliff.

The fish then went as deep as the pool allowed, and I readied myself. It leaped into the air, and as I lowered my rod tip, bowing to the fish, the salmon came down just at the top of the run where the flow went down the rapids and out of the pool.

I could see two things from this move. First, the fish was a fresh grilse of about four pounds, just up out of the ocean and bright silver, which would mean it would be very active. Second, I could tell there was no way I was going to hold the fish in the Upper Ledge Pool.

In fact, as this thought crossed my mind, the grilse went over the edge and into the rapid current, which flowed down into the Ledge Pool.

I was standing maybe a hundred yards upstream of the Ledge Pool itself, and I began to panic, wondering how I could possibly wade downstream quickly enough to be able to get the fish to turn and not have it just shoot right through the Ledge Pool to head further downstream.

I needn't have worried.

Norm, of course, had seen the entire action from down below me and was already quite prepared for what was going to happen. He was standing on the ledge, with a long-handled net in hand.

As my grilse descended through the rapids, and just as it was entering the Ledge Pool, it went close by and would have gone under the ledge itself. I say "would have" because Norm, with a move that rivalled anything my grandfather ever did, deftly swept the net from below the Ledge and came upstream, just as the grilse was coming downstream.

It swam right into the net, and Norm merely lifted the hoop skyward with the fish in it!

My first Cape Breton salmon was at hand—and I hadn't really

had to fight it at all—which might have been disappointing; but on the other hand, had Norm not done the "sweep", the fish might have headed for the open Atlantic a couple of miles downstream.

As I walked down from the Upper Ledge Pool to see our prize, I made it a fishing trip by stepping into three feet of water over the edge of the upper ledge, going completely over my hip waders, which by this time were floppily rolled down around my knees.

"Take your time," Norm said, knowing I was anxious to see the fish. "This one isn't going anywhere!"

Indeed, the only place that fish went was onto the grill, wrapped in aluminum foil with some onion and lemon slices, after we returned to Norm and Em's place. Fresh Atlantic salmon, especially the grilse, are not only fun to catch, they are delicious to eat!

10: Newfoundland flyfishing

Figure 16: Dad fishing the LaPoile River

Norma and I had been married not even a full year when Norm decided it was time to introduce me to the wonderful flyfishing that could be had in Nova Scotia's neighbouring province of Newfoundland and Labrador.

Norm's optometric practice in North Sydney had an interesting clientele, in part because of the location, close to where the ferries from Newfoundland berthed. Port aux Basques, a very small town, was the terminus on the Newfoundland side, a rather remote place for the ferries to land as the village was probably a good three hours' drive from the next nearest community of Corner Brook. As a result, many folks in Port aux Basques would simply hop on the ferry, relax for the six-hour crossing, and land in North Sydney to shop or go to appointments, like seeing the optometrist.

In any case, Norm was the recipient of a wealth of information about the flyfishing in that province. The Newfoundland clients would regale Norm with stories of fish caught, lost, or just seen.

So it was that in early July, just before our first wedding anniversary, Norma and I were packed into Norm and Em's van, and the four of us were off to see the sights of Canada's most easterly province. And to go flyfishing.

We got off the ferry and drove to Corner Brook. We picked up lunch at a takeout, where they charged us five cents for ketchup in a little pack that is generally given for free. (Everything has to be brought onto the island, they said, by way of justifying the extra cost.)

We drove to Deer Lake, where the Trans-Canada Highway (TCH) we had been following intersected with Route 430 that went north to Gros Morne National Park and eventually to St. Anthony.

Here we stopped to eat our lunch at a picnic park, and here was where Em discovered the trip might be less about sightseeing and more about flyfishing.

Em wanted to keep following the TCH and go visit friends she had in St. John's. Norm had in mind travelling to friends he had in Plum Point, which just happened to be where the Ste. Genevieve River was—one of Newfoundland's better salmon streams. Oh, and the friend just happened to be a fishing guide, as was his son.

The ensuing debate between Em and Norm took maybe a half hour, while Norma and I ate our lunch and tried to ignore the whole proceedings. Eventually, Norm prevailed and we were told to get back in the van, because we were "going North, to see the Vikings"—Norm's small compromise with a nod to tourism rather than just flyfishing.

We stopped for the night in the very northern corner of Gros Morne park, in a small campground on the banks of the Western Brook Pond, north of the village of Rocky Harbour. The regulations in those days were that sports could fly-fish for trout and salmon in Newfoundland without a guide if they were within a quarter mile of the main highway. So that evening, after we set up camp, with Norm and Em in the van and Norma and I planning to sleep in our two-person tent, Norm and I decided to explore the small river that flowed past us. Norm had heard of this spot from a client, and he very much wanted to try out this place.

On my first cast, using a small Royal Coachman wet fly, I caught a nice ten-inch sea trout—bright, silvery, and very feisty for its size, which I released. Norm, fishing just ahead of me, had also hooked a trout right away. As we worked down the stream, we repeated the "double" (the two of us with a fish on at the same time) many times.

We could see the trout in the river, for the gin-clear water was coming out of the Western Brook Pond, a large fjord lake probably two miles upstream, and fed by the glacial run-off from the table-like plateau that Gros Morne is known for. We were frustrated with the much larger fish we could see nearer the bottom of the stream, because we couldn't get a fly to them without hooking a smaller trout in the process.

Nonetheless, we had a wonderful evening of flyfishing and eventually managed to catch a couple of larger fish, particularly after it occurred to me to put on a heavier Muddler Minnow and cast it upstream, letting it drift down—much harder for small fish to hit and meaning that when it came to be below me, the fly was much deeper in the water column.

It was also a true fishing trip as I stepped off the bank of the beach at one point into what I thought was maybe two feet of water, but turned out to be more like four feet, and in any case way over my hip boots!

We kept a couple of fish each, admiring their silvery sides and brightly-coloured spots as we put them in the creel.

That night one of Newfoundland's famous thunderstorms rolled through. At about three o'clock in the morning, Norma and I had to abandon our tent, as the campground had become more like a lake, and a rivulet ran through our campsite—and right into our tent!

When the thunderstorm started coming closer and appeared to be following down the river, we both thought the captain's chairs in the van looked far more comfortable than our little aluminum-poled shelter.

The next day dawned as fresh as only a day after a thunderstorm can. In the morning, as we were standing outside the van cooking our breakfast of sea trout and bacon, a kid across the parking area was yelling, "Twenty-five cents to see the flood!" We dubbed Norm and Em's van, a large Ford F-e250 with a homemade camper top, the Ark.

That day, we drove along the beautiful Newfoundland coast and stopped at several rivers "just to see," as we headed for Plum Point and the Genevieve. Arriving at Plum Point, we found Norm's old friend Ben Coombs at the store in the motel where we would spend a couple of nights.

Figure 17: The dock at Plum Point

Ben told us he could take us flyfishing that afternoon, but Ivan would take us the next day, as Ben was already booked. Norm and I gratefully accepted, as we knew our travel partners would be patient with this arrangement for only so long.

That afternoon, Ben met us and we drove the short distance to a side road. From there, we walked across a boggy swamp that paralleled the main Genevieve River.

Norm had read in a magazine that Vicks VapoRub made a great insect repellent. We were accompanied on the walk across the swamp by what Ben described as "Newfoundland's air force," a vast number of large "moose flies," technically deer flies, a close relative of horse flies, but either way large biting insects that would tear a strip of flesh from you as they fed on blood.

Applying a liberal quantity of the sticky ointment to his bald head, Norm then smacked his hat back on. He quickly discovered that Tap, or whoever had written the "tip," was grossly misinformed when it came to Newfoundland biting insects, as the bugs seemed to enjoy the pungent smell rather than be repelled by it. Consequently, many landed on the sides of Norm's head, and when he took his hat off to swat at them, they landed like an invading force on his exposed scalp.

When Norm smacked at the stuck insects, so many spurted blood profusely that when Norm got to the river he looked as if someone had taken an axe to his head! He took a shallow bath in the stream to wash off the useless ointment, and then donned the more sensible Deet-infused Ole Time Woodsman I had been using.

We fished the couple of pools in that section of the Genevieve, but didn't get even a rise, although we did see several nice fish in the clear water. The Atlantic salmon in the Genevieve, as in many streams, can be frustratingly hard to tempt to rise for a fly, with no real rhyme or reason. Unlike trout that either hit or don't, a salmon may watch the same fly cast a hundred times and only then decide to hit. Whether it's out of sheer boredom, a territorial "get that out of here," or what, only the salmon knows. No question it makes salmon flyfishing a patient person's sport.

The next morning, Norm and I met Ivan as planned. He drove us up the 430 and then off a side road that paralleled Ten Mile Lake, the headwaters of the Genevieve River. We drove until the road approached closest to the lake, and Ivan pulled the truck over.

"We'll take my boat from here," he said.

We deposited our gear in the large wooden boat, not unlike Norm's handmade Mahone Bay craft. Ivan started the motor and we went up and across the lake, almost a third of the way along its ten-mile length. There, at the far side, and where the lake narrowed significantly, was the outflow of Ten Mile Lake, the beginning of the Genevieve River.

Reaching the far side, we got out of the boat and collected our gear again. Ivan directed us to follow a path down the south side of the riverbank.

As we began walking down the trail, we could now see, from below the level of the lake, that the pond—as Newfoundlanders call most of their bodies of still water—was held at an artificially high level by an old wooden dam. The structure, Ivan told us, had been to control the Genevieve for bringing pulp downstream decades ago, but was now roughly maintained by the salmon angling community to give the Genevieve a bit of extra protection in low-water seasons.

Any Atlantic salmon worth its salt could easily pass over, or indeed with some effort through, the old leaky dam; yet, it held back enough water to guarantee the fish run a flow to allow passage.

We walked less than a quarter mile and the tumbling river broke out into an open pool, what was termed locally a "steady." The Genevieve ran quickly from out of the woods we were walking in, went over several large boulders, and then ran a distance of maybe a hundred yards into a pool that was shaped in an almost perfect circle.

We could see at the outflow across the pool a woman angler, the only other person we'd see that day, who was just "releasing" a very large sea trout.

"Scum of the earth, I spit in your face," she said as she quite angrily chucked the fish back into the river downstream of the rock she was standing on.

Norm and I glanced quizzically at each other.

"She's only wanting a salmon," said Ivan by way of an explanation.

We could see that the pool was alive with fish. There were rises all over its surface, and it was apparent that many of the fish were of very good size.

"With all those trout in here," Ivan said, "you'll only be catching sea trout. Is that okay, or did you want to walk downstream a mile or so and try for salmon?"

Norm, who had already put his fly rod together, replied, "Oh, I think this will be just fine, won't it, Bill?"

I agreed.

At the time, both Norm and I carried our fly rods in break-down cases. Having witnessed once too often people like Dad and my brother, Bob, who put their rods full-length out the back window of their vehicle, and the ensuing *pop* as the tips got broken off when someone absently hit the rear window button, I have always appreciated the take-down case, that allows one to simply pull the fly rod in half, and then place the two pieces, with line and fly still attached, into the protective sleeve.

This meant that I simply pulled my fly rod out and noted the Royal Coachman dry fly from the afternoon before, as that's what Ben suggested we use on the salmon. It was a large fly for trout—a number 6 dry—but these looked like big fish.

It turned out that the fly size didn't matter.

As my first cast came down, carrying the fly toward the river, within seconds a very large sea-run brook trout inhaled the offering above the water's surface. Norm had a similar experience with his salmon fly, a Blue Charm that I had tied and given to him; we had a double going.

The fish I had on swam quickly out into the deeper water in the middle of the pool, and I managed to work my trout just enough downstream that it would not get tangled with Norm's. The fly line was flowing rapidly off my reel as the fish ran out into the steady, but then it stopped and I started reeling as it turned and came toward me.

"Try to get him to swim toward that little shallow over there,"

Ivan said, pointing to a small level area on the bank behind two large boulders.

I did as he said and managed to get the fish to run into the shallows, where the current was less and it would be easier to net. To his credit, Ivan was ready and he quickly netted my fish and handed it to me.

Ivan then waded into the water below Norm, who had managed to get his fish to come up just below a large boulder he was standing on. Ivan reached out the net, bringing it behind the trout, which tried to swim away, but could not because of the current, and instead was in the net instantly.

The pair of fish were almost identical. Two four-pound-plus sea-run brook trout—the largest trout either of us had ever caught.

"We'll keep these for breakfast," said Ivan. "Now go have some fun catching and releasing some more."

The limit at the time was ten fish, but this guide wisely was looking to the future and wasn't about to let anyone kill the goose that laid the golden egg. He strictly limited the trout we would keep.

We did kill one other trout that got hooked more deeply than we'd have liked, and he was bleeding. In those days, nobody had really thought about barbless hooks, but that would be the current best solution—the barbs of the hooks could be flattened so that the fish could be more easily released, particularly when dealing with large numbers of fish.

We caught and released probably fifty fish each from that pool, many of them brushing the four-pound mark, and almost all were over two pounds.

On the way back in the boat, I said to Norm, "Well, that was fun."

He grinned, and it occurred to me that many anglers might have been so intent on getting a salmon that they would have passed right by the best trout fishing one could dream of. Changing our plans and allowing nature and the fishing Guide to dictate the day's play had been a smart move.

There was one small "downer" to the day. On the way back up to the boat, we noticed that the landing area for the craft had been ill-used: beer bottles and other garbage were just back of the shoreline in the woods, and toilet paper and other signs of human encroachment were evident. Even here, in the wilds of Newfoundland, people can be so sloppy and uncaring.

I asked Ivan if we could take some of the garbage out, and he smiled as he handed each of us a garbage bag, indicating that this was not an uncommon thing for him to do. In the off-season, Ivan was a schoolteacher, so I suspect looking ahead to future generations came naturally to him.

The remainder of the trip that year was more tourism-based, which made Em and Norma happy. Norm and I did catch a few more trout along the roadways, but we knew that we'd had an experience that would stay with us for a lifetime.

~

I still hadn't caught a salmon in Newfoundland, however, and so a few years later Dad asked if I'd like to join him on a trip to a very remote salmon flyfishing camp on the La Poile River, on the southern coast of Newfoundland.

Dad had become friends with Henry through a mutual acquaintance, and I knew Henry from the Guysborough wilderness trip. Henry had found a small salmon angling experience, just starting up on the La Poile. The river is very remote, and would see the six of us guided by three Newfoundland fishing guides.

We travelled to Port aux Basques on the ferry from North Sydney, and then transferred to a small fishing boat that puttered along the south coast of Newfoundland for a few hours, until we rounded a point and entered La Poile Bay. The village of La Poile is perhaps another two-hour ride in an even smaller boat from the area known as North Bay, where a couple of old houses stood and where the La Poile River flows out and enters into the La Poile Bay. From there, one walks about three miles upstream to the camp, Salmon Hole Lodge, which overlooks one of the most gorgeous salmon pools imaginable.

The first evening at the lodge, Dad and I and our guide, Reg

Chant, went downstream to a spot now known as George's Pool—one of Dad's favourite spots to fly-fish. The pool is really a simple flat in the main current, created by two large boulders at the head of the pool. The flat water that spills below is maybe five feet deep, but is a resting spot for salmon coming upriver, as it is before any of the larger deep pools that fish would rest in overnight.

Dad told me to fish the pool first.

I had a number 4 Blue Charm salmon fly on, and I was using a 7 weight rod, so this was larger equipment than I was used to. Almost all my trout fishing is on a 4 or 5 weight rod.

On the second cast I made into the pool, I saw a silvery flash. The salmon had moved but did not hit my fly. I waited a few moments to allow the fish to return to where it had been, and carefully cast so that the fly would be swept down just past the rock and into the small flat water where I'd seen the fish.

As the fly moved past the rock, I felt a hit, and lifted my rod tip in response. The fish erupted from beneath the flat water and immediately jumped, crashing back down into the water in the middle of the pool to run downstream. I had managed to bow to the fish enough to allow the jump, but this fish was now furiously stripping line as it swam out of George's Pool and into the rapids below.

"Wade down with it," Dad said from behind me. Reg had already begun to do just that.

The fish was in a small pool just below the main pool, and was now going rapidly back and forth across the river, which meant it was fighting the current on each pass and tiring quickly. I got the line back into the reel and soon could play the fish from my fly line instead of the backing.

Eventually, the fish even swam back upstream under the rod's pressure and I got it into the lower part of the main pool. Reg was there with a net, and he got himself into position just below the fish.

"Let it swim back downstream," he said.

As I lowered the rod tip, the fish went briefly away from me, and our experienced guide effortlessly scooped it up. A fine seven-pound grilse, my first Newfoundland salmon, lay in the net.

We all gazed at it admiringly as Reg brought it up to where I was standing, still knee-deep in the river. "Nice fish," he said.

"We'll keep that one," said Dad.

I smiled broadly.

That week at the camp, I caught a couple of other salmon, Dad did as well. We also got into a large run of sea trout. I caught several trout that brushed three pounds, and each morning, after the first morning, we had trout for breakfast.

Alex Chant, the head guide and operator of the camp, provided a wonderful facility in the true wilderness—the camp had gravity-fed water and a large cook stove where some amazing food was prepared. The sports were all well looked after, and the trip was memorable for the camaraderie and the scenery, as well as the fly-fishing.

One evening on the way back from fishing one of the lower pools, Dad and I spotted a moose, which appeared to be using the trail that we were going to take to return to the camp. We decided to wade maybe three hundred yards upstream, where the bank went steeply up to the path, from where we assumed we could continue on to the camp.

Dad went ahead of me, and as he was almost at the top of the bank, I heard a muffled *whoa*. He had topped the bank and was staring a moose right in the face! The animal, with a curiosity that was obvious, had followed our progress and had kept up with us. As I watched Dad stumble backwards down the bank, the moose's massive horns and broad face looked down at us.

One of the guides appeared in a small clearing just above the moose on the path, and as he called loudly to us, the moose bolted back into the woods. It is amazing that a creature so large, with those huge antlers, can move that quickly and silently.

"You guys okay?" Alex asked.

"We are now," Dad said quietly.

Another highlight of the trip for me occurred on our final full day. Reg, seeing that I liked sea trout fishing, asked if I'd like to hike upstream to see the other pools. Dad had been to the La Poile a number of times before, so he elected not to come along; he had designs on another salmon from "his" pool.

I accepted the invitation. "Sure, I'd love to see the river."

Reg and I walked upstream another three or four miles that day, and I marvelled at the crystal clear pools in the river below. The sides of the La Poile are quite steep, as it cuts a gorge through to where it comes out at North Bay into La Poile Bay. This meant we were often walking on a small trail some distance above the stream. From this vantage point, I could easily look down into the river and see both the breathtaking pools and the many fish.

Reg had recommended I fish one of the larger pools, where I quickly caught a couple of smaller sea trout.

Reg said, "You keep fishing, I'll cook these for lunch."

A shore lunch in true wilderness is a memory of a lifetime. We had the trout, which he cooked skewered on sticks over a small open fire that would last just long enough for lunch, not the bonfire many would typically make.

Reg took a battered kettle out of his pack and dipped some water for tea, which he added by the handful into the boiling water. He also produced out of his pack a loaf of Mrs. Chant's homemade bread.

With a full stomach, we listened to the many species of birds singing on the walk back. A sighting of beavers and an osprey topped off our hike. I was thrilled.

The week had gone by in a blur, and as we sailed on the little fishing boat back to Port aux Basques from La Poile, I hoped I'd be able to get back there someday.

~

The last time I went flyfishing in Newfoundland with Norm, it was a "boys only" trip. He had invited his friend Wally along to fish with us.

When Norma and I arrived in Cape Breton, Em had stocked the Ark with enough food that the three of us could have easily stayed a month without visiting a grocery store—we were going for less than a week.

We took the ferry to Newfoundland and travelled like homing pigeons for the Genevieve. Since Norm and Wally were both in their early eighties, we made frequent stops, essentially looking at every river that crossed under the TCH on the way to Corner Brook, or under the 430 on the way to Plum Point.

We camped at the roadside just south of the mouth of the Genevieve, so that we could quickly access the river the next morning. The plan was to fish the Genevieve for three days, and then return to North Sydney in time for the sea trout run in Middle River.

The first day's fishing, Wally managed to hook a fish briefly, but the salmon got off as it brushed against a large rock. Neither Norm nor I had any luck that day.

On the second day, we went upstream, to the maximum distance from the road that we were allowed without a guide, and began fishing. After an hour or so, I saw a rise in a pool below me, but I found the water too deep to wade, so I had to wade upstream and then come down the centre of the river using an underwater point as a path of sorts. This allowed me to approach the pool I'd seen the fish in. I was now standing waist-deep in chest waders, but could make a long cast and, I hoped, cover the steady.

As I began casting, I saw another rise, again near the tail of the pool, and so I let out enough line to reach the rise, which meant I was now casting about sixty-five feet of fly line. The line would carry the fly, then would quickly sink down under the weight of the current.

I cast carefully, trying to cover the entire pool, and on the fateful cast, the fly went very deep. As I mended the line, I felt the fly stop. I tugged, but nothing moved.

Thinking I'd hooked bottom, I began pulling back with the rod tip, when the "bottom" suddenly moved!

A very large salmon had hit the deeply-swimming fly, turned with it, and was now heading downstream. It was then that my error became apparent.

I could not simply follow the fish downstream, as I would have to move upstream in order to get to the bank. From my little point of slightly shallower water, I could not simply walk to the shore, as it would be over my head let alone over my waders, so even an *intentional* fishing trip was out of the question. The only thing to do was to try to turn the fish.

I put as much pressure as I dared, but the salmon simply kept swimming, apparently heading for Labrador, and as the backing paid out much too quickly for my comfort, I could then see the spool of the reel beneath, with maybe thirty feet of remaining line.

The fish stopped, and I tried winding some line in, but as quickly as it had stopped, the fish turned again downstream.

I relived my childhood experience as I heard the reel stop and the line go *twang* as the leader, two hundred yards plus the fly line away, broke. The fish had taken the entire line and backing out and was swimming freely with my Blue Charm lodged in its mouth.

Norm and Wally had each caught a fish: Wally's a mature nine-pound salmon, Norm's a nice six-pound grilse, so they were in good spirits as we drove back to the campground. As it turned out, too good spirits.

It grew dark on the drive back toward the campsite, and I noticed a weird light in the rear-view mirror. I merely glanced back at first, and then realizing more fully what was going on, I pulled over to the side of the road.

Norm and Wally had been into Norm's flask, and were sitting at the small table in the van, playing cards—with a lit Coleman gas lantern sitting on the table between them.

"Maybe we'll just eat supper here," I said.

"Good idea," said Norm. "Let's have one of the salmon and some of these canned peas and potatoes that Em put in here."

I got out of the van to start supper.

Did I forget to mention that Norm had a little guardian angel? It was kept quite busy.

11: North River flyfishing

Figure 18: Sea run brook trout, North River

There aren't many mountains in Nova Scotia. Oh, the numerous maps of the place advise us of Kelly's Mountain in Cape Breton or of North Mountain in the Annapolis Valley, but neither is, topographically speaking, a true mountain. The term "mountain" should be applied to a land mass rising up over 1,000 feet (350 or so metres) top to bottom, and by that scale, Nova Scotia has few hills that reach the actual definition.

What this means for the fisher is that the streams in Nova Scotia are generally relatively shallow, but also rather slow moving and meandering. The Margaree, the most famous stream in the province, is just such a watershed, coming down off the Cape Breton Highlands, heading west and gaining speed until it bursts out on the riparian plain that forms the Margaree Valley. The long, slow stretches of the river are punctuated by several ripply ledges, but for the most part the Margaree is a slow mover, winding its way along the valley floor in huge S-shaped curves and oxbows, with the salmon pools situated on or near the largest of the curves.

The North River, however, is the Margaree's opposite. Coming down from the same Highlands plateau, the North River plunges down the side of the east-facing slopes, and gurgles through a narrow canyon which features a series of waterfalls before it eventually levels off just below a highway bridge, where it exits into St. Ann's Bay and flows into the Atlantic. The North River is one of the few rivers in Nova Scotia that is narrow and deep and fast. Impacted by the rain falling on the Highlands above, the North can be shallow one day and deep the next—and in that case much faster flowing!

It also is home to a wonderful abundance of fish to entice to hit a fly. The North has native brook trout year-round, and this alone would make it a fun river to fly-fish, but in addition, the North has a sizable run of sea trout—brook trout that breed in the North's far upper reaches and then find their way out to feed in the briny, cold depths of St. Ann's Bay, before ascending the North to breed once again.

These sea trout are joined by a smaller but just as exciting run of Atlantic salmon. And, just to keep things interesting, from time to time one finds a run of shad entering the river. Truly a smorgasbord of flyfishing fun!

When I first started dating Norma, her dad, Norm, took me on my first flyfishing trip to North River. The river does have one gentle stretch: just below the Cabot Trail highway bridge, the stream flattens out into a large, long pool that goes along below the old church (garnering the name Church Pool), and then exits that pool and makes two quick twists in a length of not more than 500 yards before flowing into St. Ann's Bay.

The lower section, known locally as the Tidal Pools, is where the fish first enter the river to begin their ascent, and it is the centre of some controversy. Indigenous nations in Nova Scotia are allowed to take some salmon for ceremonial and traditional use, and they use large nets to do this. Local fly-fishers object to this, and some would prefer to see this practice eliminated. The tradition exists, however, by treaty rights granted centuries ago. The nets are only temporary, and the practice is actually much attuned to the environmental impact, and the Mi'kmaw fishers take only a very small number of fish.

~

The first time I fished the North, Norm and I arrived just before dusk, and the Church Pool was our target for the evening's flyfishing. We parked the car on the shingle behind the banks of the river on the south side, where the river had made a large gravelly flat in its spring flood stage.

Walking toward the river, a rather amazing sight greeted me. The North glides down below the bridge and then runs along the north side of its bank under a rather steep three-metre-high wall of granite, just below the church, where a small side brook joins it. The cooler water from this spring-fed brook blends with the North River and the whole thing then flows along under the firm bank for a distance of about two hundred yards before the flow goes over a ledge and begins the sharp turn down into the Tidal Pools. The resulting set of pools is a series of long, wide and quite deep spots on the bank side, but shallow and very wadeable shingle on the opposite side, making this a text-book run for fly fishing. A thing of beauty.

At the top of the Church Pool, the river is also quite wide, by Nova Scotia standards anyway, maybe seventy-five yards.

This sight was enlivened by the presence of what were obviously quite large trout feeding, and of course, they were all slurping insects, right against the far bank. What this meant for the two of us, as we were alone in this mecca, was that we'd have to wade out as far as we could, and then try to get a cast over to the fish on the far side of the stream.

To make matters more interesting, the fish were obviously keyed in on the insects floating down to them, so matching the hatch was a must. A wet fly just chucked and dropped over there wasn't going to do much. (I know; I tried!)

I tied on a small, dark, dry fly, as the floating insects appeared to be dark-coloured duns. Then the fun began.

We both tried casting directly across, as that was the easiest way to get a fly over there, but that meant the current would take the fly under almost as quickly as it landed. The solution was that we had to fish upstream slightly, which shortened the reach we could have, meaning a longer cast and less control of the line.

Trout after trout rose to our offerings, but neither of us could hook a single fish. Well, that last part is not quite right, as, when we reeled in our dry flies, we would dry them by false casting and occasionally float them near our feet to see if they were dry enough to float properly, and the instant one of us did this, small brook trout fry would hit at the flies and sink them! Fun, but a little frustrating.

We kept at this for perhaps an hour and simply could not get one of the larger fish to play.

Norm finally came up with the answer. Purposely starting a fishing trip, he announced, "I'm going to get close enough to cast to them."

He began to take his chest waders off. I immediately saw the wisdom of his intended action and came ashore to do the same. In minutes, we were both wading back out into the river, only this time with no waders on, only the wading shoes that we both wore over our chest waders. The water was very cold, and wisely I had left my fishing vest on the bank of the stream along with my wallet and car keys, because to get close we had to wade armpit-deep.

With one box of dry flies in an upper shirt pocket, we approached the far side close enough to make upstream casts of our chosen flies—Norm using a Dark Montreal dry fly and I using a Royal Coachman dry (with a white forward patch of hair because it was getting dark and I wanted to see the fly).

The plan worked perfectly. On our first casts we each hooked large fish, a true double going on! The trout behaved perfectly, too, and in the large pool we had all kinds of room to play. We backed up so that the fish would come away from the bank and not put all the other trout down, and had a great time fighting two nice sea trout!

When they came to hand, mine was a two-pound beauty of about eighteen inches, and Norm's was even a tad larger. Both fish were dispatched quickly as breakfast fish, because we wanted some for a meal, and with darkness closing in, we weren't sure how many times we could repeat the trick.

We were well advised to do this, as it turned out we each hooked and lost our next trout. Both of us were also, I admit, getting chilled, so with another trout each we called it a day, knowing that Norma and Em would have trout for breakfast with us.

The warmth of the car heater was welcome on the half hour drive back to North Sydney, even if it was early July!

~

In the years to follow, I would become acquainted with the other parts of the North River. The salmon fishing on the North is better just below the first falls. One follows across the Cabot Trail highway bridge and then drives up a very rough dirt road for a couple of miles to the provincial picnic park and the paths that lead along the midsection of the river.

Norma would often join me on these trips, as she loves to just walk along the paths, look at the flowers and watch the birds, and I must admit, being in such a gorgeous locale is a big part of the tug of flyfishing for trout in Nova Scotia—the places the trout live are so beautiful, to paraphrase Robert Traver.

The North is a very clear river, except for the day immediately following a rain, when it gets all riled up. Other than that, the river is crystal clear, and from higher up the steep banks, one can gaze down into the pools and see the fish in their resting spots.

Figure 19: A Bomber fly

The midsection became a place that Norm and I would fish regularly because the native trout would be in residence for much of the season, and there was always the chance that in these pools would lie a leftover sea trout slow to ascend, or even a salmon taking its time going upstream.

One year, in late August, Norma and I visited her folks just before heading back home for the school year, and Norm suggested a new spot along North River—a much more secluded pool, but one that he had fished when he was younger, and when Norma was a small child.

Norm and I arrived about two hours before dark and parked the car on the dirt road above the river on the south side. This meant we had to go through the woods and down the steep bank, but he knew the path and located it handily, and we found ourselves at the edge of the pool, near the tail where the river ran into a series of shallows.

Norm said that he'd fish the main piece of the pool, where, just above the tail, the river ran over to the north side and again cut under a large granite face before curving out and over the ledges, then into the tail proper. He suggested that, since I liked to wade deeper, I might take the top of the pool. If I could cross, he said, I would be fishing above him and from the other side, so we'd be covering different water.

Walking carefully in my waders, I had to follow along a small cliff face for about thirty yards, hanging on to prevent dropping into the river as it bounced along under this bank, then went diagonally across to the part of the pool Norm was about to fish. I made it above the pool, and saw that Norm was right—I could walk out into the river and with some care get across and stand on the ledges on the other side.

Looking downstream, I could see that Norm already had hooked a native brook trout of about eight inches, and I positioned myself so that I could cast back to the granite face I'd just walked along.

I was using my favourite Muddler Minnow. On my first cast the fly behaved perfectly and went along under the surface, just in front of the rock face. As the fly carried downstream, it went into a slightly deeper pool just below a large outcropping of stone, and it was immediately taken by a good trout!

Raising my rod tip, I set the hook and could feel the weight of a good fish, which ran with the stream and swam into the pool below in an instant. I could not move very quickly, as I was precariously balanced on the ledges. It was a challenge to fight the fish from that position and try to get it to run up behind me so I could turn it into slower moving water in the run behind.

I managed to do just that, however, and soon had a nice, fat, thirteen-inch brook trout in hand.

That evening was typical of the North River in the late season. I ended up with a couple of fish in my creel, but caught and released probably two dozen trout, most in the ten- to thirteen-inch range. Norm had had a similar experience in the lower portions of the pool.

I worked my way down to him and saw him catch one fish that was fifteen inches in length and already had the hooked jaw of an older male brook trout.

As we started for the car, some Merganser ducks flew down the river, heading toward the bay. We spotted a beaver crossing the river below us, where he was planning on damming one of the small side streams just before it entered the main river. In the woods on the way up the bank, we were startled by the "beep, beep, beep" call of a saw-whet owl.

Cape Breton has this way of enchanting you, making sure you know it is still quite pristine with its wilderness features. Magical, really.

~

Over the years, I also fished the North alone a number of times, and one memorable afternoon stands out. I parked the car along the dirt road above the church, and bypassed the Church Pool, heading for the Tidal Pools.

Norm and I often saw fish rising in the Tidal Pools, but it is a hard stretch of water to fish properly as the depth changes completely with the tide; you have to know what it looks like at low tide to be able to fish it properly at high tide. Many folks, not knowing, are casting over blank water, where three feet away and to the side are the deeper holding pools where the fish wait for the tide to be full so that they can move up into the Church Pool and begin their ascent of the river. And a full moon is not the time to fish these pools (there are three pools below the Church Pool that collectively form the stretch), because the fish simply wait until dark and swim up during the high tide at night.

I knew all this because Norm had taught me. It was early July, and so time for the strawberry run of sea trout, so called because the strawberries are ripe in Cape Breton at the same time the sea trout begin to ascend the rivers. It was a new moon, so no light at night, and it had rained two days earlier, meaning there was plenty of flow, but the water had had time to return to its usual crystal clarity.

Approaching the first pool by coming down over the steep bank from the road, I walked past an older model tan Ford pickup truck parked just up the road from me. I carried on through the old hay-field that had been cut recently. The smell of new hay wafted by, and the sharp edges of the newly mown field grass made a whoosh sound as I walked through the stubble.

As I came within sight of the pool, I could see I was just about a half hour too early: the tide was down a bit and still coming in, so there were no visible fish rising.

As I walked to the edge of the pool, a man stepped out of the alder patch beside the top pool. "Hey there," he said, "good day for flyfishing."

"Yes," I said. "Any luck today?"

"I got my five," he said. He walked a few steps back into the alders and came out holding a stringer of five beautiful sea trout. "I was just going to take these home."

"Nice fish," I replied, a bit enviously.

The man disappeared as quickly as he'd appeared while I pre-pared my fly outfit, ran the line through the guides and tied on a Royal Coachman dry fly.

I walked absent-mindedly along the first two pools, keeping an eye out for any rises, but was sort of thinking the pools had been fished out by the other angler. As I rounded the corner of the little patch of scrubby growth, I came along the last stretch of the pools that formed a small bank along the south side of the river, just be-fore the river bent and emptied into St. Ann's Bay proper.

I became completely alert when I heard a small bloop, and then saw a large ring emerging from the far side of the river, along the bank, just under an overhanging bush. I watched and saw another rise, another large ring. I spotted a flotilla of dry flies floating downstream, and each was being swirled down and across the river and up against the bank. Every fly was being smacked as they floated along the bank, and soon the water had multiple rises at once.

I made a careful first cast, getting the fly to land close enough to the bank that it would sweep into the "strike zone," but not so close that I risked getting the fly hung up in the small overhanging brush. The fly floated perfectly, and was sucked down quickly as it passed the overhang.

Pulling up, I felt the weight of a very large trout, which took off like a shot for the deeper pool below, heading for the bay. I stepped backwards, which meant I was standing on the north-side shingle that would be high and dry at low tide, but now was covered with about two feet of water. The pool in front of me was wide and deep, and only got deeper as it went away, the perfect place to play a large trout.

The fish darted back and forth along the submerged centre of the stream, but with no stumps or other impediments to my line, I knew that I could relax and simply enjoy the action. I soon worked the fish over toward the shoreline I was now standing on and simply beached it by leading the trout up the shallow gravelly slope and back toward the alders further behind.

I had hooked the trout quite deeply and, knowing the school of sea trout could simply stop and run right through the pool any minute, grasped my prize and quickly dispatched it—a 2.5 pound sea trout of eighteen inches!

Over the next forty-five minutes, I caught and released dozens of nice size fish. I do admit to taking my limit of five, all more than 1.5 pounds each, and each one over sixteen inches—a spectacular day by any measure.

As the tide turned and the water began to go downstream much more quickly, no more rises were visible. Rather than continue up-stream to chase the school as it went along, I was content with my frantic hour of tremendous flyfishing.

I headed back toward the car.

After recrossing the hayfield and scaling the bank, I saw a man walking toward the pools, and thought with a tinge of anger that this was probably the same man I'd seen before, since what looked like the same truck was parked nearly where it had been earlier.

I got in the car, drove back to the nearby corner store and restaurant, and bought a soda. I asked the man at the counter if he knew who someone in a small tan Ford pickup might be.

"Oh," he said, "that'd be Malcolm. He's a bit of a character, that one."

"How so?" I asked.

"He'll go and catch his five trout, then take them home and come back for another five. He'll keep doing that all day. At least until he sees the warden's truck come along, and then he'll simply be fishing along the stream with no sign he's caught anything at all. Yes, sir, quite the character."

I had a very different name for Malcolm, but I didn't utter it—not out loud, anyway.

12: Middle River flyfishing

Figure 20: Middle River

There are rivers that we fly-fish that are simply things of beauty. Rivers that cause us to be happy just to be near them. Rivers that have something special about them.

Lamar Creek in Yellowstone National Park is one such river, with clear, cold water and willing rainbow trout to play with, all beneath the gaze of kibitzing bison in the shadow of scenery that is so stu-pendous it defies imagination. The Bow River in Alberta is a similar river, with its jade-green, swiftly-flowing water that is home to at least four species of trout so you're never really sure what's on the end of your line when you are fishing there; again, the scenery is spectacular.

But some rivers are special because they are much nearer and you can be fish them regularly, so you get to know them, or at least you think you do; and if they have some of those unique qualities of the more famous rivers, well so much the better.

You can really fall for such a river. It becomes Home Water.

Norm introduced me to Middle River, and I would be remiss if I didn't note that it was one of his favourite rivers as well. He'd fished the Middle since childhood, as it is quite near to the village of Baddeck, where Norm had an office and worked part-time as a sort of supplement to his main optometrist practice in Sydney Mines. He would work Wednesday mornings in Baddeck, and then take the afternoon off and go fishing. On Middle River.

The Middle is so named because it is properly in the middle of Cape Breton Island. It has some of the characteristics of the Margaree, in that it begins in the Highlands plateau above Hunters Mountain, but it then flows quickly southeast (whereas the Margaree begins by running north) down to the valley that two low ridges form, running nearly perfectly on a north/south line, and meandering a bit, like the Margaree, as it courses along and eventually flows out into the Bras d'Or, a huge saltwater lake that defines the centre of Cape Breton and that connects to the ocean through two narrow openings, one at either end.

Unlike the Margaree, however, the Middle is a bit wild and untamed for most of its length, the farms and roads having to be a bit further back because the Middle can flood, and so people give it its space. It can go down just as quickly, so you are never quite sure how much water you will encounter on any given visit, and that change is part of the challenge.

Middle River, rising from the Highlands, drains a huge volume of water from up above the valley at times, and as it flows under the bridge near the twin churches, the river flattens out over the valley floor and the water simply goes where it wishes. For a fly-fisher, this is also a rather interesting fact, because every single year the pools will change, some a lot, some a little, so you have to learn the river over and over again.

That wildness also extends to other facets of the river. Often while fishing the Middle, one is keenly observed by bald eagles interested to see if your live releases are slowed enough to provide a meal. Numerous ducks and other waterfowl make the Middle their home, as do beaver, mink, and otter. There is even the chance a moose might decide to wander down off the mountain and go for a swim, although in recent years the moose wisely stay mainly on the Highlands plain, as hunting for moose is legal in Cape Breton in the fall, just when the rainbow trout, now properly termed steelhead, ascend the river. A double, of a steelhead trout of ten pounds or so and a moose, would be a possible occurrence.

There are five fish species of interest to a fly-fisher on the Middle: native brook trout, sea-run brook trout, and Atlantic salmon native to the river, and now there are also rainbow trout and the steelhead they become.

The latter two came about by accident. The Bras d'Or is home to numerous aquaculture operations, and as some of the fish escaped, they lived long enough to find Middle River to their liking and bred, causing a new population to be present in the river. What's more, the rainbow trout, present as smaller fish in the spring and summer, become much more interesting when the sea-run rainbows return as steelhead trout and ascend in the fall as large fish.

This meshes perfectly with the brook trout fishing that is so excellent in May and June and the sea-run brook trout that ascend the river in early July, part of the strawberry run, making the Middle a flyfishing mecca for the entire fishing year.

~

I fell for the river the first time Norm took me there. We parked our car under a huge bank which was being mined for gravel for the roads, and under the watchful eye of an eagle perched high above on a large spruce, on the top of the bank.

We walked a very short distance and began by fishing a small side stream that runs parallel to the Middle and then enters the main river about a mile downstream. Using chest waders, we stepped into the small stream, which was less than waist-deep for most of its length. Even in rubber waders—this before the advent of the new high-tech material like Gore-Tex—we could easily feel the cold water.

Except for immediately after a rain, the little stream is gin-clear, and runs steadily but not too swiftly along the valley floor, confined by a small road on one side and the banks of the Middle proper on the other.

We waded downstream and, doing his best to make certain I would be appropriately smitten, Norm gave me first cast into a small pool that made a 90-degree bend as the stream hit a bank and turned toward the main Middle River below.

If someone could fish in a church, this pool is what the cathedral of fishing would look like. The small stream flowed over a gravelly rise under some alders and willows, and then broke into the pool proper. A log jutted out into the top of the pool, and you just knew the first few parishioners would be sitting there.

But the main pool that formed below was home to other residents, and they, too, could be visualized as to their lie, as there was also a large mass of underwater weed and grass that formed like pews, rows of cover for the trout.

As in any church, along the back of the pool, at the far end under the dappled light streaming through the woods just beyond, I could see fish hiding beneath the overhanging branches, just like a minister's flock—attentive but in the back of the church, holding back, as it were.

The stream exited this pool in a sharp turn, just like a side exit, and again, with a log jammed along the bank there acting as an exit path, I could actually see some early worshippers leaving.

It was spellbinding, but as I stared at the scene, a number of rises also caught my attention. Everywhere in the pool were small dimples of trout showing themselves when they came up to suck in insects as they floated down. The trout flashed in the sunlight, meaning they were sea trout, and they were quite a good size.

Carefully, because far too often fly-fishers wade where they should be casting, I let out a short length of line and dapped more than cast the Muddler Minnow on the end of my 5 weight rod under the log at the top of the pool, which was perhaps only twenty feet away from where I stood.

The flow quickly carried the fly along, and as it came parallel to the log, a large, flashing fish smacked it very quickly. I didn't have to raise my rod tip as the trout hit so hard and came down on the fly with such force that it really hooked itself.

As it felt the force of my rod and line, the trout turned and ran out into the main pool—down the left side, away from where all the others were gathered.

Until this point, I hadn't really noticed that the other part of the church, the left transept as it were, was a rather large backwater pool. It was an ideal spot, as it kept the fish I was playing away from the main pool and would not put down the other trout. It also meant I had little to worry about in the way of the fish tangling itself on a snag, as there were no branches or even much vegetation in the deeper backwater.

I played the fish for several minutes, being careful to contain it to the left-side pool, and then brought it near enough to reach with my small landing net. Swooping up from behind the fish, I was surprised to see the size—a seventeen-inch, pound and a half, sea-run brook trout. The normal rainbow-like spots of a brook trout on this fish were there, but the backdrop was a silvery hued skin, much lighter and more brilliant than any trout I'd ever caught.

I was amazed, and I was enthralled.

Letting Norm take his turn was a courteous thing for me to do next, but, I have to admit, it also let me calm down from the excitement. He quickly followed my lead and a similar fish engulfed his Grasshopper fly just at the end of the log. He brought his fish to the left as well.

We proceeded over the course of the next hour to take several fish in the same size range and a number of smaller fish—over a hundred between the two of us, I'm sure. We released all but two each. Norm did not keep his five right there because he thought he could get bigger trout in the main Middle River. I released mine because I was still in awe of the spot and didn't want to do anything to ruin the place!

We did go down to fish the main part of the Middle River later that day, and Norm did indeed catch two more very large trout in the main pool, the one that now bears his name: MacAskill Pool.

My introduction to Middle River was amazing, but there was soon more to come.

The next day, we returned and Norm thought he would introduce me to the top end of the river. He reasoned that if the sea trout were up into the side stream, they must be higher up the river as well.

It was sound reasoning. We walked in to the main river via a path he showed me that wound along the bank of the side stream, and then crossed over that stream and went a good hundred yards into the woods before coming out just above his pool.

We scrambled a bit going down the rather steep bank to the river, and were then standing at the top of a large pool that was formed where the rushing water of the Middle River came over a large shingle and then dropped about three feet into a huge, basin-like pool. Then, continuing downstream, the river formed a large narrow pool along the steep bank we'd just come down.

I could see the pool was very, very deep—maybe twenty feet—and that it went at this depth along the bank for about three hundred yards. With a gravel shingle behind, it was a dream spot to cast in, open and not too wide, and a great place to play the fish, as the pool was large and had few obstructions.

Norm said that he'd start by fishing this large pool. He pointed upstream and suggested I'd like to go up that way.

"That way" I saw another three pools roughly two hundred yards above the first pool, smaller and not as deep, but just as pretty and open. The Middle formed the pools above as it coursed out of a wooded section and then opened out onto the large gravel flats, where it carved its current flowage.

I eagerly agreed, and started upstream. I had gotten maybe a hundred yards when I heard Norm whooping; he was already playing a large sea trout.

I almost turned around to come back down, but did as I had been instructed and walked to the top of the three pools, just below the wood lot. The river there came out much like the sidestream pool, over a shingle of gravel and then up against some fallen logs.

From my vantage point, however, I could see the water under the logs was very deep, and there was no side or back pool to play a fish in. It would be necessary to cast under the log, and if a fish hit, try to steer it out from under the log and then across to my side of the river and up onto the shingle or into my net.

As I was calculating all this, a large rise showed just under the log, and I knew that Norm had been correct in his supposition that at least some trout had moved upstream.

I had put on a Royal Coachman, going with the "bright day, bright fly" mantra my grandfather used. I stripped out some line and made my first cast. The fly landed just above the log and the current quickly swept it just under the overhang.

Just as quickly, a trout smashed at the fly, and again the fish hit hard enough that my rod was bending even before I could react. I needn't have worried about playing the fish and getting it away from the log, because with the strong current flowing there, the fish was carried in an instant on the take down into the main part of the pool. I had to step downstream a few steps to keep up.

I had the trout over to "my" side of the river, and got it to come to the net after only a few minutes of frantic back and forth. The fish was a shade bigger than either of the ones I'd caught and kept the day before, heavy and thick and silvery. He'd also hit the fly so hard it was deeply hooked, so I dispatched him and got him in my creel along with some of the aquatic grass from the riverside.

Because we'd had such a great day yesterday, it occurred to me, after I had caught seven more trout, smaller but still fourteen inches or so on average and all sea trout, that I should keep track of how many fish I was catching and releasing. The total in just that one top pool was seventy-five fish, when it began to get "slow" and

I'd only hook one on every fourth cast or so.

I caught a couple dozen more in the next pool down and a dozen or so more in a quick fish down to the pool where we'd begun. By that time, Norm had gone right through the pool and had worked his way down to the main pool below.

I fished the big pool quickly, and hooked and released three more nice trout, then headed down to meet Norm. He had had just as successful a fish, telling me he'd caught quite a few, had kept four and was looking for his fifth.

I smiled as he showed me the four he'd kept, all very nice sea-run trout. He nodded approvingly as I showed him the three large fish I'd kept.

"I'll catch one more and we can go," Norm said.

I didn't have to wait long before he got another trout to take.

"This has been a pretty good day."

"Indeed," I said.

~

The number of sea trout in the Middle River in the late 1970s and early 1980s is hard to describe accurately. A story might help.

A few years after my introduction to Middle River, in 1981, the year Norma was pregnant with our daughter, my parents came to Cape Breton to visit Norm and Em. The ladies went off to tour Sydney, and, without any discussion between us, Norm and I took Dad to see if the sea trout were "in."

We drove to Middle River and to the pool above the main pool. As we were coming out of the woods and onto the path down the steep bank, we could actually look down through the clear water into the large pool; the bottom was plainly visible.

"There are a lot of weeds down there," Dad said, looking at the flowing mass on the bottom of the pool.

"There's only one thing, Dad," I said. "Those aren't weeds down there."

I picked up a small rock and tossed it gently into the pool. As the stone drifted down to the bottom, the "weeds" parted and let the rock drop among them.

The school of trout quickly reformed into their mass.

"Whoa," Dad muttered.

That day, because Dad had heard the story of fishing there the previous years, we counted, all three of us this time, and we caught and released more than a hundred trout. By this time, we were all using barbless or bent barbed hooks, so releasing the fish was easy, although it did mean that when we hooked a large trout there was that little bit of added anxiety.

In the mid-1980s, the fishing changed in Middle River, and not for the better. The Department of Agriculture allowed a local farmer to "preserve" his fields from the meanderings of the Middle River by the construction of a half-mile-long berm to "contain" the river's flow, diverting it from the winding course it normally took across the farmer's cow pasture and into a more formal, ditched stream for that section.

It never ceases to amaze me how one branch of government can allow such a thing when, at the exact same time, Trout Unlimited Canada, a couple of other local groups, and numerous volunteers were working with what was then the Department of Inland Fisheries to change the rules and protect Middle River as the premier habitat for trout and salmon that it is.

The result of the man-made bank was a dramatic change to the river in that section, limiting the habitat for sea trout especially.

To illustrate, one early July, Norm had been away on an optometrists' conference, and I was left alone to look for the sea trout and report to him the next day upon his return. I began by coming down the small side stream, fished through my little "cathedral" pool, and had caught a number of small sea trout, but none of the big fish seemed to be in the river yet.

I waded downstream to the area that was ditched. In those days the side stream became a narrow brook, but with some very deep pockets. I had to wade out of the stream in one spot, both because the stream was so deep and because it was heavily brushed on the side.

The brook had undercut a bank in a pasture and made a sharp

turn, creating a pool about the size of two bathtubs. As I was walking alongside the small pool, I positioned myself to be able to toss, more than cast, my Muddler into the centre and let the fly swirl.

As soon as my fly touched the water, a trout took it solidly and simply went down to the bottom.

The pool was so tight that the fish could not run anywhere, and so it was rather like a bobbing contest, with me pulling up, and the fish pulling down. Eventually, the sea trout yielded and became tired enough that I could slip the net under it—a two-pound fish with the shiny silver sides I was accustomed to.

Despite the tiny size of the hole, I managed to take two more fish of similar size in quick succession. I repeated this practice for a half mile or so stretch of the stream, until I reached the place where it entered the main Middle River.

The small stream doesn't meander like this any longer; in fact, that particular pool is high and dry. The stream as it parallels the main river is more like a trench in most spots, although there are one or two overhanging logs or outcroppings where small pools form and trout hold.

Needless to say, the number of sea trout now running into the Middle River is nowhere near the number that ran before. Gone are the trout congregations of four hundred that darkened the bottom like a mat. And the sea trout that remain are smaller for the most part.

Flyfishing is addictive, though, and those of us practising the art still feel a responsibility, so the various groups, including Trout Unlimited Canada, took on the ditching as a challenge. The province, in the end, did put in special rules allowing only artificial lures and flies, and a limit of three fish kept per day, with only one over fourteen inches.

~

Middle River continues to be superb for flyfishing, the sea trout do still run, and every year the upper and middle sections change as they always did due to the meanderings of the flow as it runs through the valley. Rainbow trout have joined the brook trout, and there are still salmon to be found, though fewer than before.

You can only imagine what it is like to hook a ten-pound Atlantic salmon in one of the smaller side pools on a fly meant for a ten-inch trout, and watch helplessly as the fish tears off into a deep pocket and then thrashes about, trying its best to snarl the line around something so it can tear itself loose. With just such a fish one day, I could actually see the salmon after he'd snagged my line solidly around a log; I could not reach it with my net and could not feel it any longer with the line because the fish had gone up and over the log, but I could see it was now lying underneath.

I tried to net it anyway, but in the crystal-clear water, the fish saw the net coming. With one last effort it tore clear from the tiny hook, breaking the leader.

As the fish swam away upstream, free from restraint, I thought of the wildness that is in the river still.

Last summer I fished the Middle again, as I do most summers. My friend the eagle, or possibly one of his offspring, was there to greet me.

And the little Cathedral Pool was there, but this year it was deeper because the beavers had partially dammed the flow about three hundred yards downstream. This made the whole pool deeper, which made casting and wading harder, but also gave more room for larger fish.

As I caught and released a dozen or so fish from the pool, it felt right. The river had changed again, but I was still there to see it, and the sea trout were still willing to hit a Muddler Minnow.

13: A guide and flyfishing

Figure 21: A sport, fishing the Tusket River

Braebirch, our family summer cottage in Deerfield, Nova Scotia, has a long and storied past that is inextricably tied to the province's trout fishing history. The cottage, built in the late 1880s, is on a small hilltop overlooking the glistening waters of Hooper Lake, part of the Annis River system.

In the late 1920s and through the 1930s, trout fishing in Nova Scotia hit its tourist heyday. Folks read articles in *Outdoor Life* that detailed the antics of people like Babe Ruth, who came and stayed at our cottage, then part of an extended Braemar Lodge; however, the Sultan of Swat didn't stay in the main building at Braemar, because he'd have been mobbed by other guests. Instead, his party was put up in the guide's other properties, like ours.

The story goes that the ladies stayed in my uncle's cottage, across the river from our place, and the men stayed separately in our cottage so that they could play cards and drink uninterrupted.

Growing up summering in this cottage, I was regaled with stories about guides, guiding, and flyfishing for trout. The burgeoning business of taking other folks fishing provided part-time employment for numerous relatives and residents of the area.

I have a record of one such trip taken by a cousin who guided a sport, as the people who hired the guides were called, from Wentworth Lake through to Carleton in the 1920s. They caught and released hundreds of fish and kept their limit—and then repeated the whole trip the next day!

Other stories involved huge fish and large numbers of trout caught in the wilderness on weeks-long trips to the backcountry. Albert Bigelow Paine detailed one such trip in a book entitled *The Tent Dwellers*, and this book, along with articles in sporting and outdoor magazines, helped to cement Nova Scotia's reputation as a flyfishing mecca—accessible wilderness, as the tourism promotional pieces of the time described it.

To say I grew up on flyfishing and the tales of guides, guiding, and the outdoors, then, is not in any way inaccurate. My first guided trip when I was twelve was with Peter Vacon, who had guided The Babe. So thinking of guides as people to admire and respect came to me quite naturally.

~

In 1994, I was teaching social studies and computer courses at Lockeport Rural High School, when I had the opportunity to take part in developing a new course for the province. Attending an inservice on teaching entrepreneurship to students in senior high, I became involved as a pilot teacher.

In teaching the material to the students, I realized that it would be a great exercise if I also ran a small business, so that I could better translate the various topics and threads of interest to the kids.

I looked around for a possible enterprise to undertake, and it didn't take long to settle on opening a flyfishing specialty guiding business that would run out of our home in Wallbrook, near Lockeport, but which could also take place from both Braebirch and Norma's parents' summer spot in Cape Breton.

The timing was fortuitous, as the province was just enhancing guiding, trying to up the certification required so that guides in Nova Scotia in the late twentieth century, and into the twenty-first, would be thought of as just as professional as our ancestors who were guides in the late nineteenth century.

I found out the province had just instituted a course for becoming a professional guide. The course was split in two, so one could become a Professional Fishing Guide or a Professional Hunting Guide, each requiring a four-day course and a formal exam at the end, including some hands-on demonstration of abilities. There was also a Recreation Guides certificate available in those days, which could be obtained by writing a test after one had completed either of the other two professional guides' courses.

I learned the first Professional Fishing Guides course would be held in Queens County, in Greenfield, about an hour and a half away, and so I signed up right away. This would be a far cry more than just paying the two dollar guide's licence fee that would have sufficed for many of my forbears to become a guide.

The course was everything I had hoped for, and more. We learned about the rules and regulations that apply to fishing in the province, a very experienced Master Guide addressed us about running a guiding operation, and we did hands-on course material like how to fix a small outboard engine, how to do a canoe-over-canoe rescue, and even how to plank a fish for a shore lunch.

Two parts of the course were flyfishing and map and compass work, and after these two sections, the person running the course —one of Nova Scotia's only female guides—told me that she would like to chat after the course was finished.

I wondered what this could mean, but it soon became evident, as I had scored a 98 on the written test, missing one question that I still claim was not written correctly (the teacher in me rebelling against ambiguous questions) and earned a 100 on both parts of the practical test.

As they handed out the certificates for completion, Susan asked if I'd be interested in helping to teach such courses in the future. Of course, I said yes.

I took the Professional Hunting Guides course later that year and took the written Recreation Guide's course so that I was covered legally, according to the province, anyway, to take on the business of guiding.

I later took the first Master Guide's test the province offered since the advent of the professional guide's courses, and so became the first Professional Master Guide in Nova Scotia.

~

My very first guiding adventure was, shall we say, interesting.

I had been contacted by a gentleman named Geoff, who wanted to fly-fish in Nova Scotia, but he didn't tell me much more than that. He had found my number from a brand-new website I'd put up only days before.

Geoff arrived on the appointed day at our cottage, and I met a man I would learn only later was an outdoor writer for *Field and Stream*. He told me he was very interested in catching a chain pickerel on the fly, and as this invasive species had spread into the Annis system, and were quite large, he simply wanted to fish from shore and from our canoes and boats right there in Hooper Lake.

I got him into the canoe and we paddled across the lake to where the Annis comes into Hooper Lake and makes a large cove. The weeds and lily pads cover the water near the shore there, but it does drop off dramatically, making it a perfect spot for flyfishing, as one can cover the deep water efficiently and not be casting too far.

On his first cast, Geoff landed his large black fly very close to the lily pads. The fly, designed to resemble a large leech, was made out of black chenille wrapped around the hook and the wing of polar bear fur and a sizable black tuft of marabou.

A huge wake formed behind the fly as the pickerel hit like a torpedo heading toward its target, and then turned back toward the cover of the weeds. Geoff did a good job of getting the fish onto his fly reel, and managed to get it to swim into the open water.

After the initial run, the fish didn't put up too much of a fight, chain pickerel being a bit sullen that way, and soon we had it in the canoe.

Geoff quickly measured the beast, being careful to keep his hands away from the razor-sharp teeth that a pickerel has. It was a twenty-six-inch fish with a weight of four pounds.

I carried both a tape measure and a small hand-held scale to take these measurements, as Geoff had requested these items. He also knew I was a photographer and made sure I had my camera with me, although he had his own camera in a Pelican waterproof case as well.

Geoff said, "Nice one, but not quite the one I wanted." He held the fish back over the side and released it carefully.

In the next day and a half, we repeated this scene often, but we never did get a larger fish than the first one, or at least not much larger, though several we caught were of similar size.

It turned out that Geoff was looking for a line-weight record for the IGFA, the official organization that tracks these things, and that at the time a five-pound pickerel on a six-pound tippet would have been a new world record. Geoff was already the world record holder in a couple of line classes for other species, and I learned his hobby was to try to break other class records.

At the end of the second day, we parted company. Geoff paid me, including a very generous tip, and I had a new guiding "listing" to look after—possible world record flyfishing.

Initially, I had thought that Geoff was simply a very keen fly fisherman. It pays to always do your best for every client, though. The discovery that he was more than that occurred a year later, in the spring, when I received a call from someone in Texas who essentially wanted to catch a "big fish."

The caller thought I did saltwater guiding, which seemed reasonable given that I was in Nova Scotia; but I was at a loss as to how this gentleman had gotten my name and associated it with big saltwater fish, because I didn't ever mention deep-sea fishing on my website. Although to be fair, I did mention "from shore and near shore flyfishing in the salt" for mackerel and the like.

When I asked the caller how he had found my name, he said, "Your work is written up in an article in *Field and Stream*."

I was astonished. I thanked the man for his inquiry and directed him to someone in Halifax who did fishing for sharks, and immediately drove in to Yarmouth to buy a copy of the latest *Field and Stream*. There, in an article on Nova Scotia written by Geoff, were the details of how one could fish from shore and from a small boat in harbours for striped bass, based on the conversations he and I had had during our two days together.

Figure 22: Landing a nice bass

While I hadn't made a point of the flyfishing for stripers and blues, I was enthusiastic about both, and so Geoff apparently considered that a good base for an article. He listed my name and company contact information as well as describing the work I did as a guide and a photographer.

I received calls and letters from all over in the next two months, and by the end of the season, my company, Tight Lines Guide Service, was recognized as one of the premier flyfishing guide services in the province.

I loved taking many of my clients flyfishing. Sure, some folks were merely doing a day trip and were very casual about the fly-fishing experience, but others were truly rewarding to guide, as I was giving them something they had never had before—a wilderness experience and some really good flyfishing.

Much as Pierre had done when I was twelve, I'd tell them stories of Nova Scotia and our province's past, but most times I'd also use my birding background to tell clients what sounds they were hearing and what birds we were seeing as we walked through the woods.

One such sport was a middle-aged man from Austria who loved to fly-fish, but this was his first trip to North America. He'd fished in the woods and forests in Europe, but really wanted to catch a native brook trout, such as he'd read about.

I took him to one of my favourite spots on the Tusket River. It was the end of May and mayflies were in full hatch mode.

When we parked the car, I explained we'd be walking down to the river, about a mile or so, and that we'd be fishing on the opposite side of the river from the Tobeatic Wilderness Area, the area he'd read about in *The Tent Dwellers*.

As we hiked through the woods, the thrushes were singing and the grass was the brilliant green of late spring. We saw fiddleheads along the brook that went down the hillside beside us, and the dappled light streaming through the birches, beeches, and maples gave us a feeling of calm and tranquil solitude.

When we reached the river, where the brook emptied into the main watershed, we could see from our vantage on the little knoll overlooking the pool numerous trout rising and slurping in mayflies at will.

We waded carefully into the Tusket, just above the brook's mouth, and on the first cast my client rose, but didn't hook, a nice trout. I told him he'd have to be quick because the trout were famously finicky about taking a dry fly.

Figure 23: A large trout

On his third cast he managed to be quick enough and got a hook set into a nice thirteen-inch brook trout. He swung the fish around to be just below him, and I waded out just close enough to net the trout.

Looking at the beautiful, multi-hued spots and the black skin he said, "Let's release that one. I think I'll catch more, won't I?"

I said he probably would, and we let the fish go.

He did catch more fish, and he had me put three of them in my creel, one each for his wife, his son, and himself. After a couple of hours' fishing, we began our walk uphill to the car.

About halfway back, I heard a gasp from behind me. I spun around, half expecting to see a bear or a deer.

My sport said, "Look, mushrooms!"

He asked if they were legal to be harvested, to which I replied that I was not an expert on mushrooms so I could not vouch for their species, but yes, it was legal to pick them in Nova Scotia. He assured me he was well acquainted with mushrooms and knew these to be fine to pick and eat.

When I dropped him off at his cottage rental, I saw the excitement in his young son's face as the father displayed the trout for all to see. A month or so later I received a nice letter from the family, detailing how much the sport had enjoyed the fishing and the "walk in the wilderness," and how tasty the trout and the mushrooms had been. "The trip of a lifetime," as he put it.

We who live in Nova Scotia too often take what we have here for granted.

~

Other clients provided experiences just as memorable for other reasons.

There was the professor from Florida who loved the flyfishing I took him on so much that he ended up buying a summer home nearby, and became not only a good client but a friend. I guided a young lady from Sweden who, after the fishing was over, asked me if it would be okay if she and her partner swam in the river—and then proceeded to do so *au naturel*.

And, of course, there were some who came to me fully geared up and ready to go, but who were frustrated by the Nova Scotia brook trout's uncanny wariness.

One young couple on their honeymoon was such an example. They were staying at White Point Lodge, a resort about forty-five minutes from where I lived. He was an experienced fly fisherman, who wanted his wife to learn how to fly-fish.

I agreed to guide them, and they arrived at our meeting place.

He was prepared and attired in the usual gear: jeans and a long-sleeve shirt and the chest waders were in the car.

She, however, was wearing a tank top and very short cut-off jeans. He had said she didn't have equipment, but it was early June with the blackflies in abundance; I didn't think I'd have to provide clothes!

We climbed into my truck and I drove the short distance to my home, where Norma gave the young woman some floppy jeans and a bug shirt to wear over everything, and we found a pair of hip waders for her.

I took the couple to the same place on the Tusket I'd taken my Austrian client. The couple loved the walk through the forest.

When we arrived at the river, we could see trout rising all over the pool. Since the young man had chest waders, I suggested he wade out into the main pool above the place where the brook entered to fish from there, and I'd instruct his bride to fish nearer to shore, where in the shallower water her hip boots would be sufficient.

It took me maybe twenty minutes to show the young woman how to cast and how to mend a line, as we'd fish using a dry fly, while her husband charged out enthusiastically into the main pool. She practised the ten o'clock, two o'clock motion for casting, and actually got pretty good fairly quickly, showing some natural talent for the sport. She obviously enjoyed learning the motions that would allow her to cast a fly.

Her husband of less than a week was having not such a good time. He'd waded out and was surrounded by rising fish but couldn't seem to hook any, or even get much of a rise.

I had the young woman make her first cast toward a rising fish, and as the dry fly drifted down, a fish gulped it quickly. She missed hooking the fish, and I told her to be quicker in raising her rod tip.

On her third cast, she managed to float a fly right over a large rise, the fly went down, and she reacted instantly. She played the fish well (in an open stretch of river that is one of the nicest and easiest places to play a trout that I've ever found), and we brought to hand a nice eleven-inch brookie.

She wanted to release it, over the not-so-quiet objections of her husband, but since she was standing beside me, we did let it go. She caught and kept two other fish and released probably a dozen more in an hour or so of fishing.

I asked her husband if he needed help, to which he replied with a sour look, so I simply suggested he fish the dry flies either straight upstream or straight downstream. He had been fishing sort of across the river, which meant that he wasn't getting a good drift, and the trout would not be fooled on this day by a fly that wasn't floating freely.

In the end, following my advice and seeing his wife take a number of nice trout, he did catch a couple of smaller trout, and even kept one about eight inches. But he was much less enthusiastic, his mood not nearly as bubbly as his wife's, on the trip back.

He paid me, but she gave me a very good tip.

~

Sometimes, the fates simply want to toy with you.

I had a client from Virginia who'd never caught a fish bigger than the twelve-inch brook trout that pass for monsters in his native State. He had seen the description of sea trout, and had booked a trip with me for early July in Cape Breton, when the strawberry run hit.

He had done everything he could to have a great trip—done the research, met me properly equipped and ready to go—but the weather was horrible.

He had two days to fish with me and through the rain, wind, and drizzle the first day we hit all the usual places for sea trout that I could think of. We fished North River, Middle River, and the Baddeck; we even went up into a small brook that flows down off the Highlands, thinking maybe with the run of water the fish had gone up already.

He caught nothing.

It isn't like the sea trout are always there, but to not see any trout is a rarity, particularly in early July in Cape Breton, even in the rain.

The second day, I took him over to the Margaree, where we fished the Sawdust Pile and even into the main Margaree. Still, we saw no fish.

As the afternoon wore on, the rain finally let up, and I decided as a last resort that we'd walk into the North River and fish the shelf pool between the picnic grounds and the bridge. It meant we had to walk down the steep bank in our waders with the grass slick and damp. I went carefully in front of him to make sure he could do the trip safely.

When we reached the pool, I got him to wade out to the middle so that he could cast a fly toward the bank on the other side, let it drift in the rapid current through the main pool to come below him and be retrieved through the small pool at the tail.

He fished for about five minutes and suddenly exclaimed, "I felt something bump my fly!"

"Reel in," I said. "Let's let the fish rest."

Knowing what a bump in that fast water would probably be, I wanted my sport to allow the fish time to settle back into the same position it has just risen from—most likely behind a large rock in the relative shallows of the tail pool, where the current would be slowed and a fish could rest without expending much energy.

I knew he smoked, so I said, "Why not have a cigarette?"

He lit one and smoked it quickly. After about three minutes, he asked, "Is that long enough?"

I nodded, and he eagerly waded back out to where he had stood before.

On the first cast, his large Muddler Minnow fly swung through the main pool, and as it swirled into the tail pool below, a very large fish quickly engulfed it. Line ripped off the reel and screamed as the fish tore downstream.

"Whoa!" my sport yelled, most likely just an exclamation, but it may have been meant as directional, as the fish seemed to be heading for St. Ann's Bay.

When the fish reached the shallows of the ledge below, it turned.

"Get ready to reel quickly," I said. "The fish will run back toward you."

Sure enough, the fish did, but before heading upstream it showed itself. A large, bright, silver Atlantic salmon leaped skyward and shone like a Christmas ornament as it cleared the water by four feet before crashing back down into the river.

"Holy..." my sport's words were cut short as he had to wind furiously to retrieve the line the salmon had stripped off and which was now loosening as the fish tore back upstream.

The fight went on for about ten minutes, with the salmon entering the main pool, only to then be carried downstream as it turned sideways and was pushed by the current.

"See if you can wade backwards and come nearer to shore," I suggested.

The sport did so, and soon the fish was in the lower pool. I walked out below the fish, and with a gloved hand (knowing the fish wouldn't come close to fitting into my trout net), I felt the tail of the salmon and grabbed hold.

The fish wiggled and thrashed, but I had a good grip. I brought the head up and cradled the fish so my client could see it.

"Probably twenty pounds," I said. "We have to release it, though."

"Of course," said the sport. "Just let me soak this in for a second."

"Would you like to hold it, so I can get a photo?" I asked.

"No," he said, showing himself to be a true conservationist, "that would keep it out of the water too long. Let's put him back in."

As he held the leader, I slowly unhooked the salmon and held it for a few seconds, then it squirmed and the fish was ready to go.

I let my grip loosen, and the fish bolted out of my hands and swam directly across the pool, heading back for the same spot it had come from.

"You are the greatest flyfishing guide on the planet," my client declared. "I'll never forget this as long as I live."

Those are the experiences one lives for as a guide. They make it all worthwhile.

14: Canoes and flyfishing

Figure 24: The author in Tippecanoe

The canoe is of an ancient design, used for thousands of years here in Nova Scotia by the Mi'kmaq nation. They would live in the woods from the fall through spring, using the canoe as long as there was open water. Then in the late spring, they would canoe downstream to the river mouths and the sea, staying for the summer along the coast, where the canoe was a means of transportation both to and from the camps, and also served as a fishing platform.

Most modern fly-fishers know the value of the latter: with its unobtrusiveness, being paddle propelled, and its shallow draft capability, the canoe is a perfect flyfishing platform.

Well, almost perfect.

You see, my affair with canoes has been tainted by lovers' quarrels, by cheating, and by outright danger at different times. But I have always come back to the canoe, just as any wayward lover would return to their first love. Oh, and something else you should know—this tale is about our family canoe.

When I was four, my dad thought it would be a good idea to take me for a ride in our canoe in the surf of Port Maitland Beach. I can see this same beach from my home, where I sit writing this.

Even now, the wide, sandy expanse, with only gentle swells, certainly does look inviting, from a distance anyway. The average summer water temperature here is ten to twelve degrees Celsius.

To say that Dad's idea of surf riding with a four-year-old in Tippecanoe, our affectionately-named family canoe, was ill-considered, would perhaps be too harsh, but I have heard my mother use such a term. My grandfather was a keen history student and, upon noticing the, shall we say, most defining feature of our little boat, he named the thing after a former US president's campaign theme song.

Tippecanoe is a wonderful boat with quite a history. Built in about 1912, she is a fifteen-foot guide model Chestnut canoe, probably a modified Twozer, only with close ribs for the heavy-duty work of flyfishing guiding. She is a cedar canoe, with canvas covering and two caned seats with slotted gunwales and the famous heart-shaped decks.

She came to us when my parents bought Braebirch, our summer cottage, and has stayed with me ever since.

Canoes, you should know, have certain features that paddlers love. One is called initial stability, which means that the canoe resists tipping quite well, to a certain leaning point. The classic, old-time paddlers will purposefully tip the canoe so that the gunwale is much lower on the paddling side, and thus propel the boat effortlessly through the water, by paddling on the side now closest to the water.

Another feature is called secondary stability, which is the resistance of the canoe to tipping over once it has tipped to the point of initial stability. This is where our Tippecanoe fails. Instead of gently rolling to the side and then being able to tip back upright, once Tippecanoe's initial stability is passed, she simply goes over and the passengers find themselves swimming.

In any case, with Mom watching from the beach, Dad and I paddled out through the waves and then turned to ride them back in. It was thrilling to feel the rising water start to carry the canoe forward, rapidly gathering speed as the small boat rode up on the wave. The salt spray in our faces, the wind rushing past, and the sound of the waves crashing ahead only enhanced the excitement!

The wave we were riding began to break as it was coming close to the beach, and Dad had to steer quickly with his long paddle to keep Tippecanoe going forward, since she suddenly decided that a sideways route was more to her liking.

This manoeuvre meant that the gunwale nearest the shore was now becoming lower than the offshore side, so Tippecanoe showed her natural inclination and simply rolled over.

We washed up onto the beach with Tippecanoe upside down.

Dad had been dumped out and had fallen backwards behind the boat, so he simply stood up and uttered something like, "Whew, that was quite a ride."

"Where's Billy?" my mother screamed.

Looking at the breaking waves, my parents could see the canoe, but there was no sign of their young son. Dad managed to splash his way through the breaking surf to the canoe, and he heard sounds from underneath. I was yelling for help.

Picking up the bow of the canoe, Dad managed to lift it far enough vertically to see the orange of my life vest, and he somehow held the craft aloft long enough to let me half swim, half crawl out from under the cedar and canvas death trap I'd been in.

That was my first lover's quarrel with Tippecanoe.

When I was a teen, my brother, my friends, and I used Tippecanoe to explore Hooper Lake and beyond. She was a great platform for fishing out of, for going camping in, and for generally messing about. She was not the lightest craft, as being so aged she soaked up water like a sponge, and she had shown the wear and tear of kids, and some adults, abusing her. As a result, we couldn't carry her far without putting her on or in a vehicle, but we did that, too.

Tippecanoe has explored much of southwest Nova Scotia after being launched from the top of many a car or truck. She would go routinely to places like Big Meadow or The Hedge and be launched as a fishing vessel, carrying fly anglers to places inaccessible by foot.

You had to avoid sudden moves when hooking a large trout, because Tippecanoe's temperament could bring about a sudden fishing trip if you were careless. We also learned that she is not a three-person craft, as that simply puts the gunwales far too close to the water, and makes the lack of secondary stability a very real thing, and not simply something you read about after you dry off.

~

I assumed the care of Tippecanoe and kept her at home when we lived in Wall Brook because we lived across the street from fishable water, the Wall Brook Ducks Unlimited Canada (DUC) project. I even guided out of Tippecanoe, so the circle of her history was complete.

It also led, though, to a near disaster.

My father-in-law, Norm, was fishing with me one day on a visit to our home in Wall Brook. We were fishing for the chain pickerel that inhabited the DUC project, and the best way to access these fish was by boat.

We put Tippecanoe in at the dam across the road from our home and began paddling. We caught a number of pickerel, Norm using spinning gear and small poppers with treble hooks, and me using flyfishing gear.

I should mention that Norm loved boats in general, but had not been in a canoe often, much less one with Tippecanoe's temperament. As we fished along, I constantly had to shift my weight to offset the fact that Norm was perched over to the side, which I had to counter lest Tippecanoe go over.

We fished the weed edges where the pickerel would lie, just under the aquatic weeds that bear their name, pickerelweed. On one cast, Norm cast too close to a weed patch and firmly hooked a water lily. He was pulling hard with his rod tip, but the lure remained firmly lodged.

"Stop pulling and I'll paddle you over there," I offered.

Norm heard me, I think, but he gave one last mighty pull.

It's a good thing I wear sunglasses when fishing because, the next thing I knew, the little popper was coming straight at my face. The lure hit my sunglasses with a sickening *thunk*, and the treble hook sank into my nose, about halfway up the right nostril!

"Owww," I hollered.

Norm looked back, horrified.

We hurriedly paddled the canoe back to the shore and walked across the road to the house. Norm went in first, as I went to the barn and my fly shop to find a set of fishing pliers.

My wife recollects that Norm said something to the effect of having horrible news, at which Norma initially recoiled, imagining the worst.

"I hooked Bill," he explained.

I confess, I did not share my wife's relief.

I found pliers, and also a mirror to see that the barb was clear through my nose! We drove to the hospital and the doctor who examined me asked how this had happened, to which I replied snarkily that my father-in-law had it in for me.

When the doctor gave me a shot to numb my nose so that he could extract the hook, I winced from the pain of the injection.

"Good thing you're not a woman going into childbirth!" he quipped.

At the time, I didn't really find him funny.

I lived through the experience, though, and two things came out of it. I began to only allow flyfishing from Tippecanoe, and then only with barbs on the hooks squeezed down so that if hooked they could be extracted from what they hooked, without Novocaine. I also bought a new canoe—a seventeen-foot plastic number that put another two feet between me and my sports.

Tippecanoe became a secondary boat for me at that point, as the plastic canoe was not only roomier but also had better stability, both initially and secondarily, and it was much lighter even though longer than Tippecanoe. You could also bang into rocks and other impediments and not worry about major damage to the canoe. (A cedar and canvas canoe, although rugged and handsome, does require care not to crush a rib or puncture the canvas.)

After a number of years of storage, though, I began to look at Tippecanoe wistfully, thinking back to the days we'd had. She had several broken ribs and the canvas was peeling in flakes off the outer hull. She was no longer watertight, one of the gunwales was broken in one spot, and one deck had a crack. At some point, someone had added a false keel to her bottom, a long strip of light wood that shouldn't have been there, even though someone had thought it a good idea at some point.

In short, poor Tippecanoe looked the hundred-plus years old that she was.

I mentioned this to a friend, who told me of a young man in nearby Shelburne who loved to restore canoes. I contacted Dan, and he agreed instantly to take on the restoration of Tippecanoe.

We agreed that it wouldn't be a museum-quality thing; I merely wanted to be able to paddle her again and have her be dry.

I have images of the before, during, and after, and Dan's handiwork is amazing. He began by stripping the entire canoe to its bones, removing the canvas completely. He replaced seven ribs, both gunwales, and one of the decks, and then re-covered her in a brand new sheen of canvas.

Dan then applied the proper green paint to Tippecanoe (when she was stripped we could see that she'd been repainted numerous times in pretty well any shade imaginable for a canoe) and replaced the brass bow and stern rub rails.

He called me when he was finished, and we took Tippecanoe to a nearby stream. One part of the deal with Dan was that he'd get "first paddle" in her when the restoration was complete.

Watching him lean the canoe and paddle her effortlessly was thrilling, and I took numerous photos to remember the moment.

I then took my turn. I was instantly reminded how a plastic canoe may be indestructible but there is simply nothing like a wood and canvas canoe for its ability to glide smoothly over the water. It brought me back to my youth and reminded me of all the fun we'd had in this incredible old boat.

Tippecanoe is now in my barn, hanging from the rafters, carefully placed in straps to hold her securely, where she awaits this summer, when my daughter and my almost ten-year-old grandson will come to visit. And we'll all go for a paddle.

Carefully, because with three of us...

Figure 25: Tippecanoe reborn

171

15: Cape Breton Highlands flyfishing

Figure 26: Aspy River, Cape Breton

When most people think of flyfishing in Nova Scotia nowadays, they either think of the famous streams for Atlantic salmon, like the Margaree, or they may have heard of our smallmouth bass fly-fishing which is now so popular in southwestern Nova Scotia. Some, knowing of the "alternate species," fish for shad, the poor man's salmon, or fly-fish Nova Scotia's relatively new but increas-ingly popular near-shore salt water for species like striped bass or mackerel. Most folks, though, when they think of native brook trout, believe that the "old days" of catching hundreds of trout in a day in a wilderness setting are long gone.

These folks are mistaken; they simply don't know where to look.

The headwaters of almost all the rivers in western Cape Breton rise from an area called the Cape Breton Highlands. This would include rivers like the Margaree, the North, the Middle and so on, all famous trout and salmon streams and all coming from the same source—the Highlands plateau.

In the middle of the entire western half of Cape Breton, the left lobster claw, as it looks to me on a map, there is a high, flat geographic feature that is the birthplace of almost all the rivers flowing on that side of the Island. It is a wild and barren area, with low shrubby growth for the most part, interspersed with stands of scrubby, wind-stunted spruces that are harvested rapaciously by the paper companies.

It is the home of moose and wildcat, of beaver, loons, and brook trout. It is wild. It is striking in its stark beauty. And, it is easily the best place in Nova Scotia to fish for brook trout.

Unless the wind is blowing, and then it is among the worst places on the planet to try to fly-fish.

The mountains of Cape Breton are the few real mountains in Nova Scotia, being over 1,000 feet from top to bottom, where they rise directly out of the Atlantic. As such, the Highlands create an unusual wind effect called "les suêtes." As the warm air from the east or southeast (suêtes being an Acadian term for southeast) rises up and crosses the Highlands, the air mass accelerates rapidly as it cools in the higher altitude, 1,300 feet or so, and then drops with great acceleration on the downslope along the western side of the Island. The highest recorded gusts have been in excess of 120 kph, and when les suêtes blow, it is better to be in the valleys and streams on the lower east side of the Island and nowhere near the Highlands.

On the days the wind doesn't blow, though, the Highlands are a magnificent but remote wilderness. The Highlands are so wild, the Government of Canada had the foresight to designate much of the area as Cape Breton Highlands National Park, and the road that goes around the park is the world-famous Cabot Trail. You can fish in the national park, but that requires very long hikes because, I am happy to say, access is limited, by the government's designation of the place as a wilderness reserve.

I have hiked in the park, and the fishing is worth the effort, but few people these days are up for such a challenge. The national park takes up perhaps the northern third or so of the Highlands, which means that the rest of the plateau is open to flyfishing and is more accessible, which is not to say it is easy.

Access to the Highlands is in only a few spots, where rough gravel roads have been built to allow the pulp trucks access, one good road through Hunters Mountain at the southern end of the Highlands above Middle River, and a couple of dirt roads that serve as forest fire access points. The only other road is the one I take most often, a steep scramble of a gravelled pathway, which means four-wheel drive is a must, that gives the crews at Wreck Cove access to the water containment system on the plateau.

The Wreck Cove area is home to a large hydroelectric plant, powered by the water from the Highlands directed at this point down the slopes and through the turbines at Wreck Cove. This means that above the steep drop, on the plateau proper, the water has been directed by the construction of levees, which of course also control the volume of water flowing downhill, and creates a wonderful, controlled-water-level series of lakes on top of the mountains.

The trout love the resulting watershed, and in fact, the Highlands has a higher than normal bag limit for brook trout because the Department of Natural Resources doesn't want the trout to become stunted; there are so many trout competing for food that they need to have their numbers culled and limited to grow to a good size.

~

The first time I went up into the Highlands, I was with Norm. We drove my Jeep Cherokee to Wreck Cove and stopped at the little gas station and corner store at the base of the access road, a diner and gas bar that cater to tourists driving the Cabot Trail and to the workers of the Nova Scotia Power Corporation employed at the hydro plant.

At the counter, as I paid for our fuel, I asked the proprietor about the recent trout fishing.

He said, "Oh, you'll get some."

This refrain brought a smile to my lips, as it is the exact phrase that Peter Vacon used when we'd go to Quinan to fish after our initial walk through the woods with him.

Armed with this reassurance, Norm and I headed up the hillside in my Jeep, past the gates of the power plant. As we started the ascent, we passed a small pond on the left that had some low wood surrounding it.

"Look there," Norm said excitedly. "A black bear!"

Sure enough, in the clearing right beside the water was a rather large black bear, who obviously had something good to eat and was just settling down to consume the treasure.

Black bears, being the most opportunistic of Nova Scotia's large mammals, are commonly sighted near Wreck Cove, as they find the garbage that unthinking humans leave behind very much to their liking. This means that they are not so wary of humans as most black bears would be, and instead of rarely allowing a glimpse of a bear that instinctively rushes away into the woods, these bears at Wreck Cove have associated vehicles and the humans' garbage within as a potential food source.

It does make you not want to linger on the way up the hill.

The Jeep did well on the climb up, the grip of all four wheels needed on the rough, rutted surface of the old road. I was glad I was driving, as this put me on the left side of the roadway, so I didn't have to look at the five hundred–foot drop on the right-hand side. With no guardrail and little washouts here and there, it was better not to notice the sheer drop down the canyon that had been carved out to force the volume of water down the mountainside.

When we reached the top of the Highlands, the landscape became the rather lunar-looking low scrubland that is so typical of the area.

We had a map of the woods roads that Norm had obtained from a friend, which showed the myriad trails that led off the main road, which we joined as we topped the mountain. The road from Hunters Mountain to where we joined was over thirty miles, so our trip up the Wreck Cove road, while a bit hair-raising, had saved a lot of travel.

As we turned right onto the main dirt road to go to the lake we spotted, which would be near the end of the road, a large moose impeded our drive. A female that stood nearly six feet tall slowly raised her massive head and looked at us with disdain, as if to say, "It's my road. What are you all doing here?"

We drove to within fifty yards of her and stopped the car. Neither Norm nor I wished to get out, and I'm sure we both thought of the unpredictability of moose; a story of a male moose charging a car in Newfoundland was fresh in my mind, at least.

After only a minute or two, though, she quite unconcernedly ambled over to the side of the road, then stepped off into the bog beside us and began to munch on aquatic plants.

We drove on and, after two false leads, found the small road down to the shore of the lake that was our target for the day. Norm had fished the lake before, and we could see as we pulled to a stop at the end of the road a little landing for small boats. Someone had cleared enough of the larger rocks away to be able to back a boat down to the water.

We also noticed the remains of a firepit and the inevitable human created debris that accompanies such doings. It detracted from the sense of wildness, but it was a good reminder that we all need to guard against human stupidity and the impact on the environment, whether in the form of clear-cutting pulp operations or folks leaving litter beside a wilderness lake.

The wind was not blowing much at all, and we could see insects rising from the lake's surface.

Norm began by using a small Grasshopper fly. He quickly raised and then hooked a nice ten-inch trout.

I joined him and used a Royal Coachman wet fly, as the sun was well up, shining brightly. I thought the trout would easily see the attractor fly's colours and on the first cast I hooked a fine ten-inch trout.

In the next hour or so, we each caught and released over fifty fish, and didn't walk much more than a hundred yards away from the car. Almost every trout ranged in the eight- to eleven-inch size, and all were things of beauty.

The trout were well-fed, although none of them fat and football-shaped like trout in really healthy waters are. They were nonetheless a dark colour, with the shining black skin covered with beautiful rainbow-coloured spots that define the brook trout as a species. These trout also had a particularly flaming orange underbelly, making their overall appearance something to behold.

Norm and I kept a few trout and decided on a shore lunch. We'd brought along a cast iron frying pan and some bacon and cornmeal, and I'd brought the Coleman stove that Norm and Em had given Norma and me for a wedding present. We had a kettle to boil some water for Norm's tea and my coffee, and we had brought along some granola bars, yogurt, and bananas just in case.

I soon had the bacon sizzling in the black fry pan, and the sound of the meat cooking mingled with the birdsong in the background.

When the bacon was done, I put it aside on a paper plate covered with a paper towel, then cooked the trout, already cleaned and rolled in cornmeal, in the bacon fat.

The coffeepot boiled vigorously and, before long, we were sitting beside the lake happily eating our catch. I have to say, Highlands trout consumed in a shore lunch are among the tastiest meals I can imagine, and we both felt grateful for the opportunity to be there.

After our lunch, I noticed on the map that there was a small stream that entered the lake about a half mile distant, beyond a couple of small coves, past where we had fished in the morning. I asked Norm if he'd ever fished there, and he said he hadn't, which is unsurprising. It might be hard to imagine why you'd leave the fishing we already had to go further afield.

I said I'd like to go have a look, and Norm said he was game to come along.

When we reached our destination, we could see the stream as it entered the lake was tiny. It came from another lake, a small pond really, that was within the boundary of the Highlands National Park. It flowed down quickly and came across the park border and into the lake where we were standing. It was maybe six feet wide at that point, and ran out over a series of small ledges made by the granite rocks in the area, then ran out between the boulders into the lake.

Norm went directly to the outside of me, wanting to repeat the action of the morning, so he chose to fish out into the lake proper where the stream's current was not noticeable.

I waded over the rocks to be just fifty yards or so upstream of the brook's entrance to the lake, as I could see fish rising in the clear, cold water. A lot of fish. Trout were rising, and I guessed there could be perhaps a hundred fish in the part of the stream between me and the spot where Norm now stood.

Norm was already casting and he almost instantly caught one of our eight-inch friends. Only then did he look back to where I was.

My first cast was an abbreviated one. The fly didn't ever really touch the water as a trout exploded out from underneath where the fly would have landed and hooked itself before heading back down into the stream.

I quickly got the fish into a small side pool, as I didn't want to put down the other trout, but I needn't have worried. The trout were so eager to attack anything that looked like food, they weren't paying any attention to what happened afterwards.

It was brook trout fishing even beyond what I'd experienced as a kid with Guide Peter Vacon, my brother, and Dad. It was simply amazing.

Norm splashed his way nearer to where I stood, and he too began catching trout on every cast. We lost count of how many fish we caught and released, but I was glad for the squeezed barb hooks we were using, as it made releasing the trout easy.

Again, the fish were all between eight and eleven inches, almost all of them with the same brilliant coloration as the ones we had caught on the shore where we had begun in the morning.

We kept a limit of trout each, selecting the larger fish, which in retrospect was definitely not the best decision. Nowadays, I'd keep some of the smaller ones and let the larger ones get even bigger.

The fishing was incredible, and the wading so easy that neither of us went over our boots—a rare dry fishing trip!

~

Of course, Norm and I returned many times. On one occasion, we saw a wildcat, probably a bobcat, a thin, mangy-looking beast that sat about a hundred yards away and watched as we caught trout after trout in the brook. We were both interested in the animal, but also a bit nervous. We assumed it was simply waiting for us to abandon a fish or two, or maybe it was hoping we'd clean our catch and leave the entrails behind for a meal. In any case, the sight of a large feline so close was unnerving.

In the years to follow, I took many folks up to the Highlands in my guiding efforts, and the area seldom disappointed. The "lake at the end" and the little brook almost always held fish, making it a wonderful spot to bring beginning anglers, to set the hook on a new outdoor experience.

We'd often see moose on the way up or on the way back, and many times other animals would be present as well, enhancing the overall wilderness experience. The 'accessible wilderness of Nova Scotia' was never a more appropriate nickname for such a spot.

Other times, we'd see eagles or an osprey, the birds keeping close watch on our efforts and occasionally fishing for themselves —and almost always just as adept at catching the trout as we were.

The day would never be complete without that requisite shore lunch. In the times we'd come after that first day, we made sure to bring the stove and the cast iron pan and, of course, some bacon and cornmeal. The smell of the bacon sizzling in the open air was truly mouth-watering, and when we added the cornmeal-rolled trout to the pan after removing the bacon, the new smell of fresh fish cooking was just as desirable. Freshness personified, so fresh the trout actually curled a bit, and I had to press down with a fork to make sure it would cook through.

Norm would always want tea, so a kettle full of water was on the other burner the whole time.

It made a meal that was memorable for both its taste and the setting—in the Highlands, with bald eagles circling overhead and the sound of white-throated sparrows echoing around the bush. You really could imagine yourself on top of the world.

~

The last time I fished the Highlands with Norm was as a companion to him and a group of his friends. Norm was quite excited to have three friends along for a Highlands flyfishing trip, and he co-opted me as driver and guide.

The weather on the appointed day was perfect, a slight overcast and calm winds, so, in anticipation of the events to come, we packed the Coleman and bacon, the cornmeal and some tea. Unseen by me, although past experience should have warned me, Norm also packed a slightly larger amount of his favourite beverage, a flask full of Famous Grouse whisky.

The group was composed of four eighty-plus-year-olds and their informal guide/driver. We had a wonderful drive up the Wreck Cove road to the plateau, and encountered a moose along the way —a large male moose with a huge rack of antlers standing just to the side of the road as if to say, "Yes, you are allowed to pass". The group were in a jolly mood as we approached the canals and the lake at the top of the system, and quickly got set up and were out casting their flies within minutes of arrival.

Also within minutes we had our fishing trip, as Norm, perhaps showing the result of a tad too many wee drams, stepped off a rock he was trying to stand on and did a face plant into the lake! As was his usual agreement with his guardian angel, he was not hurt, and he simply got up soaking wet. The other three men laughed, and I was relieved to see the tumble had not caused any real issue.

After an hour and a half, the anglers had caught and released many fish, and each had kept several as well. It was declared to be lunch time, and, having anticipated this request, I already had the pan on the Coleman and the bacon sizzling away.

With such a large group, I had put two cast iron pans on the stove; my thought was that the tea could wait.

That was unacceptable to one of the men, so Wally went over a few feet from me to a ring of stones and quickly got a fire going with the kettle propped up on a makeshift platform of a piece of wood that was large enough to not be consumed by the flames before the kettle boiled.

We had a lovely shore lunch, with many stories being told, some of which were probably even true. Norm looked around as we were finishing our trout and bacon and sipping the tea and said that he didn't think there was much better to be doing than what they were all doing right then.

Within two years, all of the men, including Norm, had departed this world, and I hope somewhere the group is fishing together again. It's something I think of every time I get up to the Highlands.

Some people maintain that Nova Scotia has no "world-class" fishery.

They are wrong.

16: The travelling fly fisherman

Figure 27: Pelican Pointe, Sebastian, Florida

It never occurred to me that having a fly rod and other fishing gear in my car at all times was something not everyone did. Dad, after all, had a rod and some gear in the back of the car, seemingly at all times.

I vividly remember one May, when Bob and I were small, when Dad took us to close up the chalet in Vermont for the season, and he decided to go looking for brook trout. The small brooks that gurgled down the nearby hills close to Weston, Vermont, eventually made their way to larger streams, but the brooks were perfect for wading.

Of course, with a four-year-old and a six-year-old along, Dad parked us along the edge of a pool while he fly-fished, somewhat distractedly, I'd guess, just below us.

Boys being boys, we spent our time watching things float down the lively stream, and it comes as no surprise that we came up with the idea of adding to the detritus. We crafted small "sailing vessels" out of little pieces of wood—replete with sticks for masts and sails made of paper or leaves we found lying around. Launching these above Dad meant that he got the joy of watching our creations sail past, or so we thought, just about where he was casting his fly. (This before we knew better!)

We soon got the message that joy was not what he experienced, once we were on the move, looking again for a small stream, and with instructions to "stay put" below where he was fishing anew. As we grew older, this became a more and more common practice, and eventually our fly outfits joined Dad's in the back of the car.

When we moved to Nova Scotia, I got my driver's license right away and, in exchange for doing hay pickup, vegetable sales, grain procurement runs, along with other odd chores required on a hobby farm, I had the family pickup truck, Betsy, as my own. Until then, I hadn't really travelled on my own much, but I did have the foresight to make sure that Betsy was equipped with a fly rod and some gear at all times—although I was still never quite so pre-pared as some.

Our neighbour Don Gray used to carry his fly rod and fishing gear, but also a chainsaw and chains for towing and a winch and flashlights and who knows what all—just because, if you're serious about getting to a fishing spot, you never know...

Betsy was pretty well perfect as a fishing car. I was enrolled in Acadia University, where the school year ran from September to the end of April, meaning I had May and June—the prime flyfishing months in Nova Scotia—more or less to myself, until summer em-ployment got in the way of flyfishing. With classmates ready and willing to go, we'd set off and end up down at the cottage in Deer-field, Braebirch, or maybe exploring the back roads of Nova Scotia and trying to find the best trout spots. This was not really travelling far, but it did ingrain in me the habit of always having a flyfishing outfit along.

It should come as no surprise, then, that after university, when I got married and we moved to the Lockeport area of Nova Scotia, I continued this tradition. On our own family trips, I always packed the essentials for flyfishing somewhere in the vehicle. In our subsequent travels, it was a given that we would visit spots that might offer some new fishing experience, and that I'd be prepared to take advantage of the opportunity.

~

One of our first big family driving trips occurred when our daughter, Marsha, was about seven. We drove to visit my brother, his wife, and family, who were living near Valley Forge, outside Philadelphia. When we arrived, he mentioned the brook that ran through their backyard bordered a park that had trout. I hastily acquired a fishing permit and went looking for the brown trout in the stream. I had a wonderful evening's fish, catching a number of trout and releasing them into the small, cold stream.

On that same trip, on the way home, we visited my sister in Vermont, and there was good fishing near her home as well. Just as Dad had done with us when we were kids, I parked Marsha along with her mom on the shores of one of the larger rivers, and the two of them played in the pools and looked for flowers while I played with the brook trout in the gorgeous setting that is central Vermont.

A couple of years later, we drove to Ottawa to visit Norma's aunt and her family. Norma, Marsha, and I drove in our Volkswagen van, following the Gaspé area of Quebec. (Norma's dad flew to Ottawa to join us there.)

Along the way, I procured a day permit and fished the Matane River, watching several salmon being landed almost right in the town. When we arrived in Ottawa, I told Norm of the goings-on; he made it a point on his way home to stay on with his sister and brother-in-law to go bass fishing at their summer place outside of Montréal.

All this, though, was simply preparation for the "big trip." We had told Marsha that after she graduated from high school, we'd go on a trip across Canada.

The trip was delayed by a year due to our dog becoming sick just days before we were to leave: poor Holly had cancer and had to be put down the following winter.

So, with Marsha's first year of university behind her, we began the cross-country journey.

Leaving Nova Scotia, we drove toward Fredericton and travelled up the river valley and toward the New Brunswick border with Quebec. I didn't actually fish in New Brunswick, but that evening near Fredericton we watched folks fishing successfully in the river behind our hotel.

I had agreed not to fish until we got to "new territory", though, and it wasn't until after we drove through Quebec and past Ottawa, travelling up the shores of Lake Superior, that I was allowed to begin my fishing part of the journey. It proved fortuitous that I had made this agreement.

Stopping and camping at Rabbit Blanket park meant I would get a chance to fish for the brook trout there if the weather co-operated, and thus far the trip had been quite wet. The night at Rabbit Blanket was quiet and it cleared off, and in the morning, I got to watch a spectacular sunrise on a flat, calm lake—dotted with trout rising.

I had the required fishing permits (Ontario was very good about giving visiting anglers all the necessary information), and I spent a lovely early morning catching and releasing a dozen or more nice trout. The scene with the gently curling smoke from early camp-fires, the loons calling in the background, and the sight of trout dappling the surface of the mirror-smooth lake is something I will always remember.

Leaving Rabbit Blanket, we crossed the famed Nipigon—the site of the largest brook trout ever taken, the world record for this species at 14.5 pounds, caught by Dr. J. W. Cook in 1915. The general store there has a wonderful, huge brook trout mounted over the front door, and so the memories of times past continue.

Speaking of large fish, we arrived eventually in Kenora, Ontario, home of Husky the Muskie a gigantic musky statue that sits just offshore of the park along the waterfront of Lake of the Woods, where the town in located. We stayed at a hotel on the waterfront that night as a tremendous thunderstorm went by, and ate walleye caught locally.

On television shows, one often sees folks catching and releasing fish, and frequently the shows depict folks doing a shore lunch; after eating fresh walleye, it is no wonder those shore lunches often seem to involve that species. It would be very hard to throw back in such delicious eating!

We arrived in Alberta a few days later and had storms all the way along, so not much fishing had taken place. When we arrived in Banff, we discovered there were few camping spots left, because many campgrounds were closed due to localized flooding from all the rain. We booked a hotel in town for the night.

It turned out our room faced the Bow River, which ran just past our back door. Despite the rain, I took rod in hand and wandered down to a bench in a little covered shelter beside the river, and sat watching.

A fellow fisherman came to sit with me, and as we chatted we wondered at the coincidence, as this fellow summered here in Alberta, but spent winters in Vero Beach, in Indian River County, Florida, where my family has had a place for five generations.

As we sat there, the sky began to clear and downstream, to our left, there appeared a gorgeous rainbow. The Bow, as it flows through Banff, is a beautiful shade of green, a hue caused by the silt from the grindings of the glaciers on the mountainsides above, and the water is very cold.

As we watched, the surface became dimpled with trout showing near our bank, the stream cutting from across the valley toward us, and making a left-hand turn, creating deep-pocket water right in front of where we sat.

The two of us took turns working small side pools and eddies and waded along, rather than in, the Bow, leapfrogging each other from spot to spot as we picked up both brook trout and cutthroat trout.

The pastel turquoise water rushing in front of us, with elk standing across the way and the mountains far above us to the right, the town below us to the left with the rainbow arcing overhead created a storybook scene, and another fishing travel image for my memories. I take photographs now as part of my living, and I knew I could never create an image that would do that vista justice.

Our trip continued to the coast of British Columbia. From there we came back via the United States for the majority of the route. This meant that we spent three days in Yellowstone National Park.

Now, when one thinks of flyfishing, such as the film *A River Runs Through It* made popular, the mind runs to rushing streams, with the sound of water crashing as it flows over large boulders, emptying the run into gorgeous pools of flat water where large trout await the next morsel to float past. The film was actually shot in Montana's aptly named Paradise Valley and area, just north of Yellowstone and quite near the towns of Livingston and Bozeman, where the Yellowstone, Gallatin, and Boulder Rivers all flow. I didn't have the time to do a day trip of any of those rivers, so instead I purchased a national park licence, meaning I could fish for the three days inside Yellowstone Park.

On our first evening, we parked by a small pool next to a picnic park and ate our supper in the company of a herd of bison who were wandering peacefully along the meadow. I rigged up my fly rod and walked out toward the small stream, a tributary of the larger river, and waded carefully across a backwater pool and onto a tiny island of meadow grass next to the stream proper.

As I started to cast, I realized I was being watched carefully from across the narrow brook by about thirty pairs of eyes—the bison having strolled downhill to see the curiosity of a man standing knee-deep in what was obviously their drinking fountain. The herd approached closer. I made a couple of more quick casts, and then decided that somewhere else might be a more appropriate place to fish, since the park ranger's warning not to approach the wildlife too closely rang in my ears, along with my assumption this meant not to be approached either.

The second day was our only full day in the park, and we spent most of it touring and taking in the amazing sights—the geysers, including Old Faithful, the wildlife, and the strange and wonderful landscapes that abound.

On the third day, as we were leaving the park, the road we took out the northeast corner of the park paralleled the Lamar River, a tributary of the Yellowstone. Although I had pretty well consigned myself to not flyfishing any more in Yellowstone, I did know of the Lamar's reputation as a gorgeous piece of water.

As we drove along, we came to a section of open road that was directly alongside Lamar Creek, and when we came out of a forested area, we could see a man fishing on the opposite side of the creek, not wading but standing in the verdant, pasture-like meadow on the far side of the stream.

I pulled the car over onto the ample shoulder. I meant only to take a picture, but it became evident that the man was casting a lure (a spin fisherman!) across the watershed, trying to reach our side of the river. Looking down from my slightly elevated position, I could see that the water was clear—as in I could see fish maybe twenty feet down underwater, directly below where I stood!

As I watched the fisherman opposite trying futilely to cast clear across the creek and make a good presentation, I glanced downstream from my stand and saw a dimple. Then another. Then another. There was what looked like a small hatch coming off, and behind many of the large boulders that formed the road's shoulder were trout dimpling the surface and sucking down what I at first thought must be the renowned drakes of Yellowstone, but actually turned out to be grasshoppers that were falling into the stream. The wind was enough, it seemed, to blow the hoppers into the creek from the meadow opposite, then carry them on the current across the river and up against the boulders on my side.

I looked up at my daughter and wife and didn't even have to ask.

"Go ahead," Norma said.

I dove into the back of the 4Runner for my 5 weight rod and some flies, my intention being not to even wade the river, as the bank dropped straight down into what was very deep water, but rather to scramble a bit along the boulders and fish along the near side.

As I rigged up a small Muddler Minnow, I noticed that the fisherman opposite had moved enough downstream that I would be well above him; perhaps his moving along had been hastened by the approaching small herd of bison wandering across the meadow. It seemed bovines everywhere just couldn't resist anglers and would begin kibitzing!

I climbed over a couple of large rocks and was standing, sneaker shod, on the most prominent of the set, jutting a bit out into the stream, when, as I turned to face upstream, I heard a large *gulp* behind me downstream. The temptation was just too much, and so my first cast was almost directly downstream, aiming at a large boulder about forty feet from where I was perched.

My first effort was too short, and the fly sank before it got anywhere near the target. As I drew the fly back, another rise, and another *gulp* just where it was before, a foot or two out from and almost directly behind the point of the boulder—a perfect lie for a trout.

On my second cast, I was again short of the area the fish was rising in, but again, as I brought the fly back the fish rose. On my third cast, I dried the small fly with a few false casts, being very careful not to nick it on the rocks behind me, no mean feat, if I do say so, because the wind was completely perpendicular to me and meant that on each motion, the wind imparted significant sideways drift.

Casting forward, I allowed enough line out that the fly settled softly on the water, about three feet above the rise, and perfectly aligned so that the current would drift it over the fish.

The hit was sudden and hard.

Yellowstone Park is known for several species of trout, and Lamar Creek is noted for both the Yellowstone cutthroat and some rainbow trout. The cutthroats are notoriously difficult to hook, as they tend to hit in long, lazy takes, causing many anglers to try to set the hook too early, and thus pulling the fly right out of the trout's mouth before there is any chance for it to get hooked.

The speed and ferocity of the strike this time made it obvious I wasn't into a cutthroat. My small reel sang happily as the trout sped downstream, bending my rod almost double with both the weight of a good fish and the flow of the stream.

The fish tried to dart behind a boulder, but with a quick tilt of my rod toward the centre of the river, I got it to swim like a bullet straight out into the main current. The fish began racing upstream out into the main flow. I reeled in as the fish moved further upstream.

Twice, as I thought the trout was tiring and I tried to get it to move toward the bank, it showed a reservoir of energy, swimming out once again into the main part of the creek.

Eventually, the fish began to tire, though, and, not wanting to exhaust it, I managed to get it to reluctantly float over to the boulder I was standing on and rest in the small eddy right below my feet. I didn't have a net but had enough foresight to have put my landing glove in my kit.

Slowly I dipped my now gloved hand into the water to wet it, and then I grabbed for the trout below me. The fish didn't move, tired from the fight, and so I had brought to hand a beautifully silver rainbow trout of about eighteen inches.

"Nice fish!" I heard from across the creek.

My daughter took a couple of pictures of me while I played the fish and one of me holding it, and then I released the trout carefully back into the Lamar.

A gorgeous fish in a gorgeous setting—what travelling with a fly rod is all about.

17: Flyfishing in heaven

Figure 28: Cousin Don, Cloud Lake Wilderness

The wade downstream to the Cathedral Pool on Middle River was a bit maudlin this particular year. Norm had passed away the previous summer.

I was almost to the head of one of his favourite pools, and as I looked out past the large log that jutted out to my right, I smiled because I could see a trout rising there, just past where the current flowed out into the wider expanse that made the pool proper. I thought of how many times Norm had waded to this precise spot, and how he'd often end up hooking the end of the log or one of its side branches, trying to get the perfect drift of a fly into the flow to cover the pool properly.

It's a regular occurrence now, and not just on the Middle, that I think of the people I've fished with who are no longer there to share with me the beauty and peace that the rivers bring.

I cast my Muddler and, since it was a grey day, I used my grand-father's mantra, "dark day, dark fly."

As the current carried the fly just past the log, I saw a large splash, then felt the weight of a nice fish having taken the fly. The line zipped out across the pool, but the pool was so small that the fish simply turned after about twenty-five feet and swam in a sort of arc around the far end, as if swimming in a pond. The Cathedral Pool has a shallow as it makes the hard right turn, and while the pool is seven or eight feet deep at the far end where it flows down-stream after hitting the bank opposite, it shallows considerably, and so the trout simply don't react and race downstream as one would think they might.

After a few laps around the pool, the fish, a good-sized sea trout, simply sulked on the bottom of the pool. I continued to put pres-sure on him with my 5 weight fly rod, and eventually got the trout to swim into a shallow area with a gravelly beach leading down into it. Not even needing a net, I simply beached the fish quickly. I meant to keep the fish so that Norma, Marsha, and I would have sea trout for breakfast.

As I fished that morning, I caught and kept two more sea trout, enough so that each of us had a breakfast fish. A sort of homage to Norm, who loved to eat trout.

We fly-fish to be out in nature. To be one with the streams and the wildlife. So flyfishing is a solitary pastime. And yet, it is the times with fellow anglers that come to mind just as frequently as my solo adventures in my pursuit of peaceful recreation. When some of those friends and relatives are no longer around, the fish-ing changes forever, although it goes on.

It is different.

~

Two years after Norm died, my uncle Don died at age eighty-three after being hit by a car as he was crossing a street in rural

Wolfville, Nova Scotia. On a snowy January day a year after that, my good friend Steve Adams passed away. Recently, I was cleaning out my fly-tying desk when I came across a bunch of Muddler Minnows Steve and I had tied the last time I tied flies with him.

Figure 29: Steve fishing for shad

Steve's wife, Brenda, was my administrative assistant when I was the director at the school board, and one day she introduced me to her husband. Steve and I had formed a bond instantly. We discovered we both loved flyfishing (funny how one finds that out almost immediately about someone), and we cemented the discovery by going out together on Steve's boat to look for smallmouth bass, a species which has taken over a lot of habitat from our native brook trout in our area of Nova Scotia.

It was the kind of evening that shows if you really will get along with someone, as the fishing was superb—but the blackflies were thick! At one point, the back of Steve's fishing jacket (a "bug proof" number with a little hood on it) looked like someone had rolled it wet in pepper; he was covered.

I was covered with the blackflies myself, and had enough Old Woodsman repellent on (made up of Deet and pine tar) that folks could probably smell me before they could see me. Since the fish were hitting, I was having a great time anyway, but I worried that Steve might change his mind and bring us ashore.

Steve reeled in a large bass, and with a big smile said, "Boy, isn't this great!"

I needn't have fretted. In the vernacular of the southwestern shore of Nova Scotia, Steve was as "fierce" a fly fisherman as I, probably more so.

Steve and I fished together often after that initial trip. We discovered a lovely trout stream nearby that few others seemed to be aware of. We both revelled in the finding, and our friendship further cemented when I learned that Steve didn't like to keep more than a few trout either. We gleefully went along our new-found little stream, catching and releasing dozens of trout along the way.

I even took Steve to the Billy Hole one night, which I suppose, looking back on it meant, we really were close friends, since I took very few local people, outside of my family, to the spot. He was as enamoured as I was with the pool, and the night we first went there together there was a hatch on; the trout were showing all over that section of the river.

Again, we must have caught and released fifty fish apiece, but I don't think either of us kept a single one. It was flyfishing at its purist, just the two of us, the river, the trout, and the odd interloping duck or loon that flew overhead.

To be waist-deep in water, at almost eye level, as it were, with the trout, with a good friend fishing alongside, is great fun. To have the experience and have trout willingly take is special. To add in the whispering whistle of black duck wings or the plaintive cry of a loon as they pass elevates the experience to magical.

Steve introduced me to some fishing spots as well.

One winter's day, he arrived at my office to extend an invitation. He said he and a few other guys often went salmon flyfishing together, and while they had in the past gone to Maine, this year they were going to fish the Matapedia River in Quebec, because one of the men had just purchased a small cabin there. They'd be going the first week of July; would I like to come along?

I said I'd have to ask Norma what she thought, as it would mean I'd be gone for the week, but I also was thinking that it meant I'd miss the prime part of the sea trout run in Cape Breton.

The next morning, I called Steve and said, "Sure, let's do it!"

Steve and I drove together to the camp on the Matapedia, stopping in Campbellton, New Brunswick, to pick up some supplies and then in the village of Matapedia to purchase the required licences and passes to allow us to fish the river.

The Matapedia is a storied salmon stream of beautiful clarity and with a run of large salmon that is simply amazing. It is also the site of some rather interesting rules. In purchasing the licences, we had the choices of either 'catch and release' or 'catch and keep' and 'public' or 'private' water. It turns out that the Matapedia has superb fishing in water that is privately owned, but to gain access to this private water, one must pay a steep fee—$700 or more per person, per day to fish the very best pools.

Steve said we'd only be fishing the public water, so we got off relatively easy and paid our fee of $75 a day for a "catch and keep" licence.

Figure 30: Matapedia glory

When we arrived at the camp, I discovered the reason for Steve's keenness to go on the trip: the camp was located across the road from one of the very best public pools on the entire river.

Steve introduced me to the other men, all friends of Steve's from past experiences, and I realized I was being accepted into a group of people who meant a lot to Steve.

The next morning, we got up early, had a quick bite to eat, waddled across the road in our waders and boots, and slid somewhat clumsily down the bank to enter the waters of the Matapedia.

The pool we were fishing was just above an old covered bridge that spanned the river. Upstream, the river made a lazy turn to the left as it entered our pool, having coursed down some very impressive hills to our right. There was a mist on the water that morning as it had been cool the night before, so the whole scene was like something out of a fairy tale.

Figure 31: The Matapedia Bridge

We fished that morning and, while neither of us raised a fish, we did see three fellows from France, who had flown to Montréal and driven to the Matapedia for the salmon fishing, hook a beautiful fish.

The reel screamed as the fish shot downstream, then went silent as the fish jumped. That salmon was well over twenty pounds, and the sight of such a large fish jumping and running upstream was incredibly exciting. The men fought the fish quite hard, the idea being that you want to catch the fish quickly so you can release it unharmed and not exhausted, or the salmon will break free.

These gentlemen had another idea, though: they'd purchased a catch and keep permit for the day as well, and they were intent that this would be a keeper. The beauty and peace of the sport was shattered as the three essentially gang-tackled the salmon and dispatched it with blows from a rock!

But, the salmon was a thing of beauty, silver and fresh out of the sea—and it weighed twenty-seven pounds!

That afternoon, Steve and I fished a pool just downstream from a beautiful covered bridge, the famed Heppel Pool. Steve made it a fishing trip to remember.

With just the two of us there, he said I should fish the near side, where there was a nice open beach of sand to wade out on, and he'd take the far side, where the shrubbery came right down to the water's edge, but one is casting to the pool with a much shorter line. This was not purely altruism on my partner's part; he simply wanted to cover the pool how he thought a fish would respond the best!

I waded out and was lazily casting my Blue Charm, covering the near side of the pool, and Steve had positioned himself where he was standing on a rock jutting out from the bank on his side. After a couple of minutes, it happened. Steve's cast had swung his dry fly just out of the main current and along a "seam" where the fast current slowed, and just beyond a large underwater rock. A perfect salmon lie.

The fish that came after his fly was huge—perhaps bigger than the one we had seen in the morning, and it swung viciously after Steve's fly.

Three things happened all at once. First, the fish missed the fly, because its rise so surprised Steve that he sort of stepped awkwardly backwards, causing him to pull the fly away from the salmon's take. Second, because he was standing on a rock and one can't just step backwards off a large boulder, Steve started to fall backwards.

It was one of those graceful, slow-motion deals every fly-fisher is familiar with. You lose your balance, you start to fall back, and so your reflex is to reach out and grab whatever is handy to stop your fall. In this case, that meant Steve grabbed a handful of overhanging alder branches, which slowed, but did not stop, the inevitable. Steve got wet.

Third, to add insult to injury, the fly was wrenched with such force back toward Steve, that it struck him in the right forearm and hooked him!

In my defence, I did ask Steve if he was okay, but I admit that I expressed my concern between what he described later as "gales of laughter." He assured me he was fine, but then we both noticed the fly line draping from his arm.

In the flyfishing guide's course I teach, we go through how to release a hooked angler, so I did as trained and pressed the eye of the hook down, with a loop of line around the bend of the hook and counting to three, I pulled on two.

Eventually, Steve forgave me, but in the moment, he did not seem as grateful as one might have assumed. His major concern was whether the number 6 Bomber he was fishing was still useful —because he was going to go right back out and try to raise that fish again!

During the trip that week, we had remained fishless, and so on the fourth day we decided to venture closer to the outlet of the Matapedia, where it joins with the Restigouche, and where there are five or so public pools. To get there, we drove down a side road that paralleled the Matapedia for most of the way down, which passed the Section 2 pools, the private water. The expensive water.

As we drove along, we saw in one pool a sport and a guide sitting in a flat bottomed boat, covering the water from a seated position. There was a car parked along the side of the road overlooking the pool, that we pulled in behind to watch the action of the more affluent angler.

As we got out of the car, a smiling, blond-haired young man of maybe seventeen years struck up a conversation. He told us how his dad, in the boat, was going after his second salmon of the day, as he (the youth) had already caught his two.

"You want to see?" he said, far too eagerly. "They're right here."

The kid opened the rear hatch of the car and there were three beautiful salmon. "Took us all morning to catch these," he proudly proclaimed.

As we drove away from the scene to head downstream to the public water, Steve made several disparaging comments about the wealthy and how advantageous it would be to spend the $700 each for a day on the river. I was less kind and mumbled something about flattening tires, or alternatively, cement overshoes.

That afternoon, though, Steve did catch one salmon—a gorgeous ten-pound adult.

He kept it.

The last time I fished with Steve was in the late summer, on his boat; we were flyfishing for smallmouth bass. Steve and I had gone three times together to the Matapedia, but this year, I had said I'd not go, as I wanted to fish the sea trout run in Cape Breton. I had had a wonderful trip to Middle River and the Margaree, and had caught some very, very large trout.

Steve had gone to the Matapedia and met up with some of the group from years before. During that week, he caught seven salmon and raised or released a half dozen more. It had been a spectacular week for each of us.

On this September bass fishing trip together, as darkness began to creep across the lake, Steve hooked a large bass, bigger than either of us had caught that evening. In our brief late-evening trips like this we often kept score as to the most fish or the biggest fish, and Steve didn't like to lose. As he brought the bass alongside the boat, we could see it was nineteen inches or better, and would easily be the biggest fish of the day.

I asked if he'd like me to net it, but not really waiting for the reply, I swooped overboard with the net—and missed the bass.

Worse, I hit the leader, and the fish got off. I think Steve always thought I might have done that on purpose.

During that fall, Steve's prostate cancer, which had been diagnosed the previous winter, worsened. It had metastasized. Just before Christmas, Steve passed away.

And so, three of the most important men in my life are no longer with me. They are now with my grandparents and all those others I mourn, yet remember.

~

Uncle Don and his son Donnie, my cousin, used to go every May for a canoe trip into the wilderness area of Annapolis County, near where their family has their cottage. The spring after Uncle Don died, Donnie called me to ask if I'd be interested in doing the trip with him.

I felt the passion in his voice even through the phone, and instantly replied, "I'd be honoured."

On the appointed day, I arrived at Donnie's camp before lunch, and we loaded his old aluminum canoe on top of my 4Runner. We drove the few miles to the small dirt logging road that veered from the main road and wound through the forest down to where the brook we were going to fish exited from a fairly large lake, then coursed downstream through a series of pools and rapids before joining an even larger lake about six miles downstream.

We untied the canoe and carried it basket style (one of us on either end, the equipment in the boat) down to the stream. The carry was easy, only about a hundred yards, but as we stepped down the path, it felt like we were entering a true wilderness. The overhanging spruce trees, interspersed with the large pines, were making a *swooshing* sound in the light breeze of that May morning, and as we got closer to the small river, we could hear the gurgling water.

When we came out of the woods to the river's edge, we saw across the opening a pair of loons swimming about on the pool's surface. They quickly flew off, their flapping wings making a staccato sound against the water until they got airborne.

The smell of freshness was everywhere in the slightly-damp air. The scent of the grass, as we pushed through the small marsh to the actual stream, mingled with the odiferous ferns and the faint scent of the early apple blossoms. We disturbed a bullfrog, who croaked his disapproval when we pushed the canoe into the dark water.

Looking downstream and out into the small pool where we had launched our craft, I could see the current carrying out maybe forty yards, but I could also see trout rising! Donnie suggested I give a couple of casts over the pool, and on the very first cast I hooked a feisty, ten-inch brook trout. It would be the first of many that trip.

As we paddled downstream, we had to fish carefully because the canoe did make some noise, being aluminum, and the trout, while plentiful, weren't stupid. We used Donnie's aluminum craft rather than my plastic or cedar canoes because the stream there is so rough. Open and deep in places, it becomes a mass of boulders and lovely little runs. Great for trout fishing, but hard on the water-craft!

At the first of three portages, as we brought the canoe across a small point of land to put it in again below the rapids, Donnie said we needed to get out, wade onto some rocks, and fish this particular pool carefully. I said he should go ahead and show me, sensing that he was trying to tell me something.

Donnie clambered out onto the largest upstream boulder (we were both wearing sneakers, as this was May, after all, and we were making it a fishing trip on purpose!). On his first cast he rose but did not hook a large trout. Casting quickly out again, using almost a roll cast to avoid the trees behind him, he managed to get the fly forward and right over the rising fish. It hit instantly.

After playing the fish for several minutes, Donnie was all smiles as he brought it to hand. "This was Dad's favourite pool," he explained. "In his later years this is as far as we could come. He loved this."

On that particular trip Donnie and I each caught and released well over a hundred brook trout. In the years after this trip, he and I have done a May trip every year, and have done this exact trip almost every time, although together we now also have found a few other spots nearby that interest us and still involve long canoe rides with short portages and wonderful trout fishing.

Some years we catch a lot of trout, some years we catch a few. Some years we are ahead of the blackflies, and some years we pay the price for mistiming and have to share our trip with myriad biting guests. But each time we go, somewhere along the way, we'll stop and remember Uncle Don and talk about how he loved just such a fishing trip.

~

For me, the same holds true when I go to the little brook up the road that Steve and I discovered held trout. I think of Steve and how he loved the stream, but most of all how he just loved being outside.

I think of Norm when I go to Cape Breton and fish the Middle or the Margaree and of how he, too, loved to fly-fish and loved so much to find the places the trout live. I think of my grandfather every time I fish the Culvert, The Hedge, or Big Meadow.

You see, flyfishing is a solo pastime, but with reflection it becomes about tradition and those times spent with people who shared a love of the outdoors and a love of the creatures that inhabit those special fishing spots.

Many of these places are described as being "heavenly."

I believe they are.

18: Flyfishing in the salt

Figure 32: Indian River Lagoon

The year after Grampy Carl, my mother's dad, died, I found myself living with my grandmother in Nonquitt and working a summer job to pay for university. This arrangement was so my grand-mother could have help while she was "summering alone," but it became a wonderful opportunity for me to begin to gain some in-dependence. Of course, it also involved fishing.

When I arrived at my grandmother's summer home, situated in

a small village just south of New Bedford, Massachusetts, right on the shores of Buzzards Bay and overlooking the Elizabeth Islands, Martha's Vineyard, and Nantucket beyond, I learned that the striped bass and bluefish were running.

The family owned a small wooden pram, and I asked Aboo (our nickname for our grandmother) if I could take it from the garage down to the shore and tether it there. With a smile at the familiar request, she agreed, so the Billy Bob was at rest on the north beach. Years earlier, Dad would have rowed Bob and me out to the ledges off the beach, where he would have surf cast for stripers and blues, while we boys would help net the fish and occasionally get to toss a pencil popper lure out ourselves, under Dad's watchful eye. This time, I was on my own, using a fly rod.

~

I have been fishing for striped bass almost as long as I have for trout. When I was nine, I caught my first striper in an epic battle that is recorded in my dad's diary.

We had picked up friends from the airport, and Dad decided to tour them around. Naturally we went around the Chebogue loop, going from Yarmouth toward Rockville and then around to Arcadia. We stopped to point out the island our family owned, and since everyone was out of the car anyway, Dad took out his bass rod and wandered to the edge of the river.

The banks of the Chebogue, a tidal river, were fairly steep, and the eelgrass gave way to mud in places where the river was below half tide. Even now, the smell of a salt marsh and the mew-like cry of gulls circling overhead instantly bring to mind days like this.

Dad cast his two-ounce pencil popper maybe a dozen times and declared there wasn't much going on. As he turned to go back to the car, I was standing beside him and asked if I could take a cast or two.

"Okay," he replied, "but be careful of those hooks."

I made an initial cast of maybe ten feet, the lure barely touching the water, and everyone had a good laugh at my lack of skill. Perhaps egged on by what felt like raucous derision, I took much more care on the second attempt and made what Dad described in the diary as "a pretty good cast." High praise.

The popper had gone out maybe forty feet, and it was in the centre of the river. I started to reel in and, as the line came tight, I "twitched" the lure with the rod tip and the lure responded by making the *pop* in the water—the sound that it is named for— making little circles spread out from the head of the floating fake fish.

The water beneath the lure erupted.

A large striped bass savagely hit the pencil popper, turning on the lure and taking it underwater briefly. I reacted with a trout fisherman's reflexes and jerked the rod tip up.

Three things happened at once. First, the fish was hooked. Solidly. Second, because I had brought the rod tip up quickly I was leaning backwards. Third, I lost my footing, falling onto my back in the mud and was being dragged feet first toward the river by the fish as it rushed away.

To my credit, it is recorded that I "kept my calm" and managed to hold on to the fishing tackle and began to reel in, as the fish would alternately swim away but then turn and come toward the shore. All this from a prone position. Eventually, I managed to get to my feet, the fish tired, and I got it ashore.

Dad waded out, getting soaked in the process. But he stated, "It was worth it." He beached my first "on my own" striped bass—a ten-pound thing of wonder.

~

With that as background, I had in mind striper fishing with a fly rod while at my grandmother's place. The idea was actually quite simple—the Billy Bob, affording me the necessary reach, would be stationed on the north beach just in front of her house. From the deck of my grandparents' home, I could see when stripers or blue-fish were chasing bait, and when this occurred, I had noticed the baitfish often got pushed up into the shallows of the bathing beach by the predator fish, which meant a school of bait and feeding fish were visible as the whole group of fish worked along shore.

One afternoon, we were sitting on the deck. Just as Aboo was settling in for her evening cocktail before supper, I spotted the telltale sign of ripples in the water.

I hollered, "Fish!" and ran for my casting rod, already set up with a small blue pencil popper, and my fly rod, ready to go with a large Clouser Minnow tied to a 12 pound test leader and a short length of 50 pound test—because there could be bluefish out there. That precaution turned out to be prescient.

I bolted for the pram. Flipping the Billy Bob upright, I threw both rods in, along with two oars, and shoved the released boat into the bay.

As I began to row toward the large rocks that define the north beach, I saw the ripples still working toward me and was very excited to see that the action had now caught the attention of a circling flock of terns, who were now diving into the schools of fish below.

Once I was in position to intercept the mass of fish as they came within fly casting distance, I false-cast a couple of times, getting about sixty feet of line out, using a hauling cast but not letting the fly hit the water, and finally let the fly go forward and down. The cast was good, reaching the middle of the ripples that indicated the school of baitfish.

Almost as soon as it hit the water, I felt a hit. Raising my rod tip slightly, I felt the weight of a good fish, and knew instantly what I had hooked as the line screamed off the reel.

Bluefish tend to go in a single long run away from you when they are hooked, while striped bass tend to take, go out a bit and then sort of zigzag back and forth. This was definitely a bluefish.

The blue was taking line off the reel at an alarming rate. In trout fishing, backing is used more to fill out the reel and make the fly line wrap better, the backing filling up the rest of the space so that the ninety feet of fly line is wound more loosely around the centre spindle. But when you're fishing large gamefish such as salmon or saltwater fish, the backing gives the angler an extra couple hundred yards of distance to let the fish play.

This time, the bluefish turned before he took off all the line, and I began playing it and reeling in. The fish fought hard, taking several more short runs, but I did get it up to the boat, only to realize I hadn't brought a net!

Bluefish are known for being quite aggressive. The blues school behind the baitfish, then when the conditions are right, they just swim through the school with their mouths open and cut the baitfish to shreds. Blues, you see, have *very* sharp teeth!

Since there was no way for me to reach down and bring the bluefish into the boat, I did what any kid would, I simply held the fly rod with my knees and rowed the short distance to shore.

Once on the beach, I hopped out of the pram, reeled the rest of the line in, and slid the bluefish onto the shore. It was a lovely blue of about fifteen pounds.

My grandmother received it eagerly and declared we'd have it for supper the next night. I was thrilled—my first bluefish on a fly rod.

Later that summer, my parents came to visit me and Aboo. Of course, Dad heard all about the bluefish.

We got up early one morning to go to the south beach, south of the bathing beach where we had seen a school of fish working earlier the day before. The dawn was one of those typical New England mornings: the wind was light and soft, and the salt air was delightful. The sea was also almost as smooth as glass, with a slight break just as it came ashore, the small waves making a *whooshing* sound as they broke on the hard sand, then a *rrroooosssshhhhh* as the small pebbles were rolled backwards and pulled toward the ocean.

We saw gulls and terns overhead, and a great blue heron stood just down the beach from us, watching intently as Dad and I waded into the water.

Dad had his spin casting outfit and a pencil popper, and he cast out not even forty yards. I had the same fly outfit I'd been using all summer—a 7 weight weight-forward line with a Clouser Minnow tied to a short leader and the 50-pound test tippet to avoid having a bluefish bite off the fly.

As Dad worked his lure back in toward the beach, we saw the rush behind it. A large fish was following the lure as it popped along. Dad kept reeling in until the popper was within about twenty yards of the shore. I had already gotten out about sixty feet of line, so I false cast my Clouser out five feet behind Dad's lure.

It was then that the excitement intensified!

The moment my fly hit the water, a large fish rolled right on top of my fly, and at the same instant, an even larger fish hit Dad's popper. We had a double going—of sorts.

My fish took off, heading for the open ocean, so I knew I had a bluefish on. Dad's fish, obviously a good-sized striped bass, went straight sideways, intent on breaking off by swimming into the rocks where the road was protected by a bank of large boulders.

We each gleefully fought our prizes for a few minutes. I got my blue to slide up onto the pebbly beach, which allowed me to grab the landing net out of the car and swoop Dad's striper. The pair turned out to be a nine-pound bluefish and a fourteen-pound striped bass.

We caught and released a few more fish that morning, but I learned a lot, committing to memory the idea of having a casting rod to "toll in" saltwater fish to entice them within fly-casting range.

~

Saltwater flyfishing became even more important to me when my wife and daughter and I could afford to go to my parents' place in Florida on school March breaks. Our family has a condominium in Sebastian, Florida, just north of Vero Beach—about halfway between Miami and Cape Canaveral on the east coast of the state.

What makes our family spot so wonderful is that it's located on the shores of the Indian River lagoon, and is immediately across the river from the Pelican Island National Wildlife Refuge. Pelican Island is just inside the barrier beach that runs from Palm Beach all the way to Cape Canaveral, and the inside forms the Indian

River Waterway.

There are five large "cuts", or inlets, in the Indian River barrier beach, where the salt water comes through a narrow opening and refreshes the river, which has a small tide as a result. One of these cuts is just north of our place, across the river at Sebastian Inlet, so we see the influence of this quite dramatically.

While the river looks like any freshwater stream, instead, Indian River is teeming with any fish species that likes either salt or fresh, because the brackish water can be quite salty near the cuts like the Sebastian Inlet, or quite fresh further from a cut, near the mouth of one of the freshwater rivers that also enter the waterway.

I go down every morning we are there, which is now a longer stay thanks to retirement, and by simply walking onto the marina banks or boardwalks, I can cast to a wide variety of fish. We have seen porpoises and manatees in the marina most years, but we also see sea trout (actually spotted weakfish), crevalle jack (known locally as Jacks), snook, and redfish. Some years, the bluefish come in, and I've caught ladyfish and gar, hooked a tarpon, jigged a sting ray, and even landed a flounder on a fly.

Figure 33: A jackcrevalle

A few years back, a friend took me out in his boat. We were

anchored fishing one spot, which was like a depression in the river out in Pelican Island. We had a blast as we caught an Indian River grand slam of snook, redfish, sea trout, crevalles jacks, and ladyfish all in one morning.

Figure 34: A snook worth catching

He used a fly rod, but he also had along a spinning rod. When the rate of hits slowed down, Terry suggested I hold on to my fly for a second, while he plopped a plastic shrimp imitation weighted lure with his spinning outfit into the hole. He made one twitch on the retrieve and hooked a large redfish.

"Yep, they're still there," he said.

We caught and released maybe a dozen fish apiece in the next hour or so. Great fun, and again, that spinning rod had come in handy.

Figure 35: A Clouser Minnow for salt water fishing

~

There are also times that you can be in competition with spinning outfits. I've used the technique of a lure on a spinning rod to draw fish closer when fishing for mackerel in Nova Scotia. The idea is that you cast out the small lures normally used for mackerel, and when a school comes close, you can then toss a fly out there.

This isn't surprising, as the old-time mackerel lures used to be three-ounce lead weights with a hook, which sat below a "mackerel rig" of five or so brightly coloured flies, all strung together on a hand line. Drawn vertically in the water from a boat or wharf, such a combination is deadly on mackerel.

But mackerel are also incredible fun on a fly rod. One evening in Lockeport, the mackerel were said to be in. I wandered down to the wharf in Jordan Falls and saw a number of my students fishing there. They were all using spinning rods, and they were catching fish, buckets full, in fact.

So, I set up my 7 weight and joined them on the shingle along-side the old wharf pilings. At first, the kids were amused by my apparent lack of knowledge about what a fly rod was for—trout, they thought—but when on the first cast I hooked and had quite a tussle with a good-sized mackerel, they took notice. I caught a dozen or more in the hour that I stayed and took home my own bucket full of fish for suppers to come.

The next day in school, I smiled when I overheard one of the kids telling the tale of the mackerel fishing. "There was old Mr. Curry" (I was all of thirty-five) "with his fly rod. He cast back, and it went KEEE-RACK...and then went out there. And he CAUGHT A MACKEREL!"

"It actually looked like fun, you know..." stated another, almost wistfully.

I think they all thought I was slightly deranged, but they did give me kudos for using a fly rod and catching saltwater fish.

~

A spinning rod is not seen when you fish for the most prized of saltwater gamefish—the bonefish.

Norma and I have vacationed in the Turks and Caicos three times on a gorgeous beach on Grace Bay, located on Providenciales, one of the larger islands in the chain. It is also home to some spectacular bonefish fishing. I had hired a guide the first year we went, and he took my father and me to the lagoon areas just off North Caicos. We stopped the boat in a mangrove-lined tide pool that was almost encircled by the vegetation, so there was no wind at all.

The guide asked me to stand on the bow platform and cast out. I did as requested, then he poled the small boat from the rear platform that gave him a little elevation to spot fish from.

He said, "Oh, there's one at about ten o'clock, but I don't know if you can reach him."

I spotted the fish from where I stood and made a quick cast that landed just to the left of the fish and slightly in front of it. The fish turned and hit the fly ferociously.

I set the hook and we were into the fight of a lifetime. That bonefish circled the boat at least twice and made several start-lingly quick runs that ripped line off the reel. I loved every second of it, and as the guide helped me boat the fish, its silver sides glistened in the intense sunlight.

It wasn't a huge bonefish, maybe five pounds, but the play of that fish, in those shallow water conditions involving sight casting to a feeding fish, was exquisite.

After a couple of quick photos, we released the fish gently.

The guides in the Turks and Caicos take their time with the fish and treat them like gold, because they are so valuable as an income source, and also because the guides in the islands know the con-servation of such a species is honouring their ancestors.

I wish we all thought that way.

Figure 36: A weakfish

19: Flyfishing with the next generation

Figure 37: Theo's first brook trout

My daughter, Marsha, and I were having a wonderful morning paddle up the small stream that locals know as Little Meadow

Brook. The trip was special even before it began: it was the last time she, as a single woman, and I would paddle and fish together.

As we paddled that morning, I was thinking more about the past, how my little girl had worked hard and became a gifted student, graduated with high honours from my alma mater, Acadia University, and was now a law student about to get married later that very same week. It was nice just to have the time alone with her before she began a whole new stage of her life.

Of course, it was also nice because the fish co-operated that morning.

Marsha, having indicated that she'd like to be the guide that morning, had taken her seat in the stern of the canoe; I got the fishing seat in the bow.

Before we even had the boat in the water, I could see trout rising. In my first couple of casts, I managed to hook and catch a small brook trout, which we both admired before I released it gently back into the brook.

A good omen for the day.

The paddle upstream on this particular brook is not long, maybe a mile and a half, but one is traversing water adjacent to the Tobeatic Wilderness, so it's about as wild an area as one can get in Nova Scotia. As we rounded each small bend, we would pause to survey each small pool beyond, looking for the telltale sign of dimpling water that would indicate a trout or two.

Little Meadow is a very small brook, so the fish are not large as there isn't enough forage to grow really big. Besides, the large fish migrate into the main Tusket River, just where Little Meadow Brook flows under a beaver dam and out into the larger river. In each of the first half a dozen pools, I caught and played trout, all about eight inches in length but fat and feisty, and a lot of fun on a light 4 weight fly rod.

Marsha paddled softly, propelling the canoe forward slowly so as not to create a ripple, and she commented on how much she loved the sound of the lily pads as the canoe brushed along the channel. There was no wind, and the light fog made the morning feel tranquil, with birdsong and the running water providing the soundtrack. We didn't actually talk that much on the trip upstream, as we both basked in the experience of being close to nature.

When we reached the main pool above the beaver dam, there were several nicer fish showing. I cast carefully and caught two eleven-inch trout before the commotion put the fish down; the games for that pool were over.

We turned the canoe toward home, and now the paddling would be very easy as we could just drift with the slight breeze and run the canoe back upstream. This meant that we chatted more, and relaxed as we spotted birds and even found the odd trout still in the pools we'd already floated over.

When we got back to the car, we both knew that we'd shared a very special day.

Four days later, I walked Marsha up the aisle of the chapel at Acadia University, the very place my uncle Bob and aunt Carole were the first couple to be married in, and the place where I had met my Norma years before. With family all around, Marsha and her husband, Josh, felt the familial bonds tying us all together. They were beginning their life together, while Norma and I were at a new stage as well. Watching our little girl grow into her own person was cause for pride and reflection.

~

We introduced Marsha to the outdoor life very early on. We have photos of her as an infant on my back in a pack, accompanying us on hikes—of course, some of those hikes entailed fishing. We have images of her on skis at age three, cross-country in our end of the province; but she also learned to ski downhill when she was six. She sailed at an early age with me in our little sailboat, and even went duck hunting at age four (let's just say it was opening day of the duck hunting season, Norma was in the hospital after a back injury, and, well, the rest is really self-explanatory). And she also learned to fish.

Marsha's first few trout were on spinning outfits with worms and were really almost mirror images of my experiences. She had witnessed flyfishing, of course, including one incident that stands out in my memory.

We took a visiting teacher salmon fishing on the LaHave River, and Marsha came along and "waded" the side of the river while her mom was looking at flowers. The image of her at four years old, in shorts, a large floppy white hat, and pink rubber boots that came to just below her knees, standing waist-deep in the water, with a huge smile on her face as she tried to spot salmon, is one I won't ever forget.

When Marsha was ten, the opening day of trout season would be her first genuine try using flyfishing gear. After an off-season of practice casting in the yard, she was ready to try it for real.

The day dawned bright but cold, so Marsha and I elected to go to a small pond near our Wallbrook home. When we arrived, we found the pond almost frozen over, but the edges of the water were thawed, and in places there was enough of a pool to cast carefully with a fly.

I set Marsha up on the first such section of water, and then I waded out a bit further, as I had hip boots on, whereas she had only knee boots. I caught a nice fish of about eight inches, which I showed to Marsha before we released it—as we treat all first of the season trout—and we both commented on the fish's brilliant colours and its plumpness.

As I returned to casting, I noticed that Marsha's fly line around the reel was tangled a bit. She managed to get the line onto the reel and was reeling in the slack, when she lifted the rod tip and saw that her Mickey Finn fly was swimming quite rapidly away from her, out under the ice!

Raising her rod tip in a very professional manner, she hooked her first "on her own" fly rod trout, which fought hard as it ran out under the ice, threatening to snap the leader on the edge of the hard surface. Marsha tilted her fly rod slightly and eventually tired the fish and got it to swim toward her.

Just as I came alongside her, she simply stepped back and slid the fish up onto the icy shore. Her first completely unassisted trout, eleven inches of beauty!

Marsha took to flyfishing as something she liked to do with me, although she also enjoyed going along for the walks, as does her mother. One beautiful summer's day when Norm and I were fishing the sea-run trout on Middle River, Marsha, about thirteen, and Norma were along for the walk. Norm and I were doing well, having caught and released numerous trout, both native brook trout and the larger sea-run brookies we were keen to fish for.

While Norm and I were wading in the river and the ladies were making their way on the banks, soaking in the gorgeous scenery that is Cape Breton in July, the four of us rounded a curve in the river. We had arrived at the top of one of the best pools on Middle River—Norm's Pool.

As we approached, we could see numerous trout breaking the surface of the water and sucking down dry flies and nymphs, especially at the end of the pool below us. We also spied a pair of fishermen at the tail of the pool, perhaps a hundred yards away.

The two gentlemen looked like Orvis had thrown up on them—they were outfitted with Gore-Tex waders, the stocking-foot expensive kind, and had flyfishing vests bulging with every contraption known to humankind. They had Orvis rods and reels, and each had on an Orvis cap. Obviously, the State of Vermont owed these two something for their consumerism.

Later, when we chatted with them, we discovered they had gone through the heart of the pool too quickly, intent on the sight of the large fish that always show at the tail of this pool, but which, unbeknownst to many, lie almost all the way along the pool, if one fishes right next to the far bank.

Knowing we'd be far enough upstream that we weren't going to bother the anglers below, Norm and I handily worked out line and cast across the river and downstream with our Muddler Minnows, and each of us was instantly on to a trout. Mine was a small native brookie, fat and a beautiful dark black with spots that almost danced on its sides. Norm brought to hand a fine sea trout, a fourteen-inch male with silver sides and the same pretty spots, which almost twinkled in the sunlight.

We released both fish, and as we worked down the pool, we

caught and released fish almost at will—sometimes the smaller dark fish that live in the river year-round, and sometimes the bright migrant sea trout. We had travelled about halfway down the pool, when Marsha spoke from behind me.

"Dad, can I give it a try?" she asked quietly.

"Of course," I replied, pleased that she wished to fly-fish with us.

In an instant, Marsha stripped down to her bathing suit, which she wore under her shorts and top, and put her sneakers back on, intending to wade wet and fly-fish. She took my rod and worked out line nicely, casting to the far bank and downstream, and hooked a nice sea trout on her very first cast.

Over the next half hour, there was my daughter, in a bathing suit and sneakers, completely out-fishing a pair of well-equipped anglers who had simply gone through the pool too quickly.

A few years later, I think to please me but also because she had some interest, Marsha joined me as I taught a Professional Fishing Guides course for the province. Marsha passed the course and became one of the few female guides in Nova Scotia.

At the time, I was running my flyfishing business, Tight Lines Guide Service, so it was helpful to have a female guide on staff.

Marsha got to meet Susan Veinot, another of the guide instructors, and a superb and experienced hunting and fishing guide. Susan and Marsha bonded over the weekend-long course, as Susan imparted a lot of wisdom to all the participants in the event. The tradition of guiding runs deep in this end of Nova Scotia, and women have been an important aspect of the work. Marsha and I discovered later that a nearby neighbour was actually the first certified female fishing guide in Nova Scotia.

I do appreciate that my daughter shares my love of the outdoors. Even though Norma doesn't fish much, she loves the outdoors equally. It is truly a family affair.

~

Marsha gave birth to a son in 2012. I immediately started planning fishing trips for grandson Theo. When he was four, his mother and

I took him out in the rain to dig worms, which we attempted to use at a local spot in a howling east wind and spitting snow and rain. The event quickly turned into playing with sticks; no fish in their right mind were going to be about on that day.

During the summer, though, I took Theo in my large kayak and we paddled around behind the graveyard in Port Maitland with fly rod aboard. The smallmouth bass that have taken over this system are good fighters, and although it pains me to not be able to fish for trout here any longer, the bass do make for good beginner's targets.

Theo and I made a great afternoon of it, with me casting out and hooking a bass, and then passing the rod to Theo, who gleefully played the fish in to the boat's gunwale. He was enraptured by the look and feel of the glittering scales on the pretty bronze side of the fish. He enjoyed watching them swim away as we released those we caught.

All was well with the world as another generation was hooked on flyfishing.

A year or so ago, Marsha and her family came to visit us at the family place in Florida. The very first morning, Theo and Marsha joined me at the wharf to watch me, Grampy, fish. I caught a small redfish, and Theo remarked that it was a "very nice fish." We didn't manage to hook any more, so he didn't get to fight one on his own, but that's for another year.

The juxtaposition of generations is not lost on me. I am now Grampy Curry, to Theo at least, and of course it brings back memories of those who taught me in the past. Dad is now ninety-six and doesn't fish anymore, but two years ago he took a spinning rod down to the lake in Deerfield on a summer's evening and tested the waters, hooking the pickerel that have invaded the watershed. I can recall the many days he'd take us flyfishing for trout, and I remember having done the same for Marsha.

I am thrilled to be able to pass this on to a grandson. And I know my brother Bob does the same with his son, Asa, and his daughter, Erin, both of whom are now married and who have made Bob another Grampy Curry.

It is important to pass on the love of flyfishing, as it is through this sport that the outdoors draws many in to become conservationists, or at least people who just appreciate and thus care for the outdoors. Beyond the fishing, I am thrilled to hear Theo ask about bird species and admire flowers and trees.
We need people who value and care about nature. We need more people who fly-fish.

20: Flyfishing: hope for the future of our planet

Figure 38: Trout rising

I am sad.

We are back home and it is a beautiful early-summer day, so I go to one of my favourite fishing spots on the Tusket River, a pool named for me, the Billy Hole.

Family history has unfolded here, a place my great-grandfather fished, my grandfather fished, Dad fished, many uncles and great-uncles fished, my brother and I both fished, and our offspring have fished. It is a rare pool in that you reach it by hiking a mile-long footpath.

It is a remote pool. It is above Kempt, in the upper reaches of the East Branch of the Tusket River. It is a bonny piece of water, as Norma's ancestors might say, and over the decades, like many members of my family, I've landed countless trout here, most released, a few taken home for a breakfast.

Ever since I discovered as a young teen the exact spot that bears my name, it's been among my favourite places to fly-fish for brook trout.

I walk through the woods, which today are alive with birdsong and the smell of newness in the air. The recent rains have made the path fresh and the air crisp.

I find myself at the familiar look-off, a parting in the spruce trees that line the banks of the river, giving it a spruce-filled scent that lingers as one enters the stream. It's a place where in the past I've stood and counted dozens of trout rising at the same time.

Today, despite perfect water levels and ideal weather, nothing is showing. In the past, such an occurrence was rare.

I wander down the little side brook to fish the pool where that small rivulet enters the main river, forming the Billy Hole.

On my first cast, it happens.

I feel the strike of a small nine-inch fish, and bring it to hand.

A chain pickerel.

Heartbreak.

I knew this day was going to come, I was just hoping it wouldn't come so soon. I was hoping my grandson, Theo, could fly-fish for trout here in a few years, and become as engaged by the river and the trout as I have been.

Chain pickerel, the smaller cousin of the northern pike, are a top-of-the-line predator. They eat anything they can stuff in their mouths. They destroy trout directly by eating anything smaller than themselves and by eating many things the trout also feed on.

Pickerel are invasive. They are not native to Nova Scotia; they are imports. And it was humans who put them in the Annis and Tusket Rivers, destroying the trout.

Unfortunately, once the pickerel get into a river system, there's not much you can do to stop them. They thrive in the now warmer waters we have. You'd have to poison an entire watershed, and even then one idiot and a bucket and they'd be back.

It sickens me to see the spread of pickerel, and I'm frustrated today because it means they are only a mile or two below the Big Meadow Brook Trout Unlimited project we've been working on for a dozen years.

I go up to the project on the way back and catch and release a half dozen trout. That is good news, as it means the pickerel aren't there.

Yet.

But just two years later they would be.

Humans have this desire to remake the world into what they think is a better place—for themselves. They do so without thinking about, or possibly even knowing, the consequences, although the science is clear and available for any who care to look. Climate change stares us in the face; yet, in the United States, for example, the climate change deniers win power, keeping in motion the seeds of environmental destruction.

These changes will negatively impact all of us as the rain acidifies once more and the temperatures warm. The gullibility of those who deny, bolstered by fake science in their own little bubble world, creates a flow of constantly-reinforced selective falsehoods, all designed to allow things to continue as they always have, even while science says we are killing the planet.

Here in our locality of Yarmouth, a shift has taken place. There are many fewer trout.

And that is what makes me sad.

~

I also have hope, though.

In the early 1990s, Norman Maclean's novel *A River Runs Through It* became a movie. The film ignited a kind of fashion for flyfishing. At the time, I was running my flyfishing guide service, so the film was a timely boon, for suddenly many folks wanted to try their hand at the sport. The enthusiasm was also good for the outdoors in general.

The more people experience sports like flyfishing, the more they care about nature. This type of activity is beneficial, as these activities draw people to an area where they spend money and increase economic activity, but the people engaged in such pastimes don't have a huge negative impact on the environment.

Many don't seem to understand that in such pastimes as flyfishing, birding (or bird watching, as some call it), and outdoor photography, those passionate folks who take their interests outside become champions for the planet in general. I was fortunate enough to have caring ancestors who made certain I understood the aspects of nature that were important to them, but those teachings also inspired me to become an activist when it came to caring for the environment.

The very first Earth Day was in 1970. I was living at the time in Groton, Massachusetts, and about to leave to live permanently in Nova Scotia. A wonderful group of people had become very concerned with the fate of the Nashua River—rated at the time as one of the ten dirtiest watersheds in the United States. Led by Marion Stoddart, groups formed to try to rectify the situation.

My own little part in the effort was to begin an environment club at my school, Lawrence Academy, and to ask questions of the companies that were polluting—including the company my grandfather, my mom's father, Carl Lawrence, owned. He chaired the Groton Leatherboard company.

Spurred on by my grandmother, Carl's wife, Lucy, I presented a letter to him and the board on behalf of the LA Environment Club. To our amazement they not only listened, they agreed to act on the proposals that Marion had helped us draft.

Today, the Nashua (and the tributary that runs through Groton, the Nashoba), is clean enough that the fish have returned, and people can swim in it—a testament to the groups that cared enough to make a difference.

Groups like Trout Unlimited in the United States and Trout Unlimited Canada have made a significant difference to the water quality in North America. On Earth Day 2005, I and a group of like-minded anglers founded the Tusket River Chapter of Trout Unlimited Canada. We help educate youth about the river systems in south-west Nova Scotia, and improve habitat in the rivers we live on, and were given responsibility for the Provincial River Watch program, in which we trained people to be good stewards of the rivers, and how they could help educate, and report if necessary, people who violated Provincial fishing laws.

The vast majority of members in these groups are people who fish, many of whom fly-fish. I sat on the National Board of Trout Unlimited Canada for three terms, and was on a Provincial Inland Fisheries advisory board for decades—with fellow anglers who had the betterment of habitat in mind so that fish populations could thrive.

Governments are becoming more and more aware of the economic benefits of green tourism related to watersheds and the environment—and soft tourism (for the most part non-consumptive and simply "people being out there") is becoming known for its benefits, both to the participants and to those who work to keep such places as pristine and wild as possible.

~

Unfortunately, in Nova Scotia we face other challenges as well.

Even before the 1970s, the large steel factories in Canada and the United States spewed pollution into the air and caused acid rain to fall over the entire northeast of North America. Nova Scotia, situated to the north and east of many of the steel-making areas, was the recipient of the acidification, turning our rain acidic.

With limited buffering soil available in the western mainland of the province, the rivers became inhospitable first to Atlantic salmon, then to the native brook trout, and then to other aquatic-based organisms such as frogs and mayflies. In the late 1980s, Canada and the United States took steps to mitigate the pollution, but the damage here had been done.

To make matters worse, smallmouth bass and chain pickerel, both invasive, non-native species of fish introduced by human activity here in Nova Scotia, began to spread, by natural means (going in flood stages through previously unaffected watersheds) and by illegal human stocking. Some folks did the latter because they thought it better to have a fish to fish for, thinking that the trout had died out.

Once the bass and pickerel were introduced, these people were proven correct by a self-fulfilling action, and it is to the shame of every "Johnny Pickerelseed" that these fish are now prevalent through much of mainland Nova Scotia. With climate change and warming summer waters, the situation only worsens.

In Cape Breton, though, we can see a glimpse of what is possible. The soil there is buffered by the lime deposits and gypsum that abound, so the trout populations never got quite as low. And the water is cooler in the northern end of the province, making it less hospitable for bass. Even here, though, there are invasives present, as the powers that be allow aquaculture in the Bras d'Or lakes, and escapees—mainly rainbow trout, another non-native invasive species—reproduce upriver, pushing out the native brook trout.

However, the government has stepped in, and we see special limits on some streams and adjusted fishing rules to allow the brook trout to thrive as much as possible. In the Highlands there is still exceptional fishing for small native brook trout, and there is still a good run of larger sea trout. This status is protected by sci-entifically-adjusted regulations on some of Cape Breton's rivers.

That's all good, and the fact there are people working to make sure the trout can thrive is also good. The same situation, despite the challenges of poorer water quality and invasive species, occurs in other parts of Nova Scotia.

Even in the very southern end of the province, where pickerel and bass are most wide-spread, there are streams that run directly from a source through to the sea, and so do not have any lakes large enough to have attracted the illegal dumping of the invasive fish. These streams are making a bit of a comeback as those of us who know of them jealously guard their actual location, and work quietly to improve the watersheds so that the trout and other native fish in them might increase in number.

The efforts are paying off, there are places one can take a youngster to where they can catch a trout—and learn about the fun to be had with a fly rod and catch and release fly fishing.

Going forward, I would hope for more good things.

On one recent annual wilderness canoe trip with my cousin Donnie, we had a hard day to fish with high wind and high water; but in the last hour, when the wind dropped and the sun's warmth emerged, a pool we were paddling through came alive with a mayfly hatch and the rises of perhaps a hundred trout. Such sights give me hope.

I hope that Theo will get to fish for wild, native brook trout in his home province. He has already caught his first trout all by himself, and he shows intense interest in all things outdoors. I hope he will travel places and be enamoured of the beauty around us.

I care about this deeply. I know his mother cares just as deeply. I hope he will care just as much.

It is up to each of us, though, to care enough to do something. Join Trout Unlimited. Write letters to your representatives. Take part in environmental efforts like Earth Day and clean-up days. Recycle.

Do it so that, in the future, our descendants will say we did care. Do it so that you can fly-fish with your own children, and their children, too. Do it for a love of nature and the planet we cohabit with all of the wondrous life on it.

Great Grandmother Sarah Fry was right: "Thou has received from thy Creator, and not a little from thy ancestors, gifts for which thou art responsible."

Bill Curry

Acknowledgements

Thanks for the concept of this book go to my daughter, Marsha, for the idea and the push to write all these stories down; and to my wife, Norma, for agreeing to let me write in addition to all the other things I do. The book is an obvious thank-you to my siblings, who feature in many of the stories, for them putting up with my shenanigans as a youth and now as an adult; and to my parents, who did a marvellous job of allowing three kids to grow and to be curious, enabling us to become the nature lovers we all are today.

I owe much to the people who helped me with my writing: Sandra Phinney for always encouraging the written word, Paula Sarson for the tough job of helping me polish the book before sending it to be looked at by publishers, and finally to the great team at Moose House Publications, who agreed to undertake the book as a project—publisher Brenda Thompson and my wonderful editor Andrew Wetmore, who helped me craft the book and who, without changing my voice, offered many suggestions and improvements. All have been amazing people to work with as I produced this work.

I also owe much to my ancestors—the ones I knew, like my parents and grandparents, but also those who came before them. Many were farmers and dwellers in rural Canada and the United States, and they lived with the land, including the waters they depended on for their livelihoods.

I hope these stories inspire consideration of our future, for the sake of the brook trout locally and for our planet's sake globally!

Bill Curry

About the author

Bill Curry worked as a photographer and writer for many publications and media while attending Acadia University, and after graduation began his long career as an educator. Bill taught every grade level from Primary to Grade 12 in public schools, and Bachelor's and Master's degrees courses in three universities. He spent most of his career as a classroom teacher at Lockeport Rural High School before becoming involved in a two-year federal education program. Later, he became a Consultant and finally a Director of Programs and Student Services in Nova Scotia's former School Board system.

Bill became the first certified Professional Master Guide in Nova Scotia when the professional guide certification program was created, and for almost two decades ran the Province's premier fly-fishing Guide Service, Tight Lines Guide Service. Bill is also a former National Director and life member of Trout Unlimited Canada.

Bill is a Master Photographer, having studied formally in New York City. He holds a Master's degree in Fine Art Photography. Bill's photography strives to stir people's imagination, reminding folks of time spent in our shared environment.

Bill's work has been shown in Canada, the US and in Europe, and has won many awards. Bill has his own photography gallery and studio in Port Maitland, NS, where he teaches and sells his photography. His work is also shown in galleries across the Province.

Bill and his wife, Norma, and their dog, Sam, live in Port Maitland, and travel as much as possible—always with a fly rod along for the ride, just in case.

Bill has written and produced photography for numerous magazines, newspapers and other media ranging from the New York *Times* and the Boston *Herald* to *Canadian Fly Fisher*.

Tight Lines is Bill's first book.

www.ingramcontent.com/pod-product-compliance
Lightning Source LLC
Chambersburg PA
CBHW061147120626
46546CB00005B/1960